59 STORIES

NOVA SCOTIA'S
Curious Connections
TO THE REMARKABLE
the World-famous
& the Strange

from "History With a Twist" author

Bruce Nunn

NIMBUS
PUBLISHING

Nimbus Publishing Limited
PO Box 9166
Halifax, NS B3K 5M8
(902) 455-4286

Printed and bound in Canada

Design: Margaret Issenman
Author photo: John O'Donnell

Library and Archives Canada Cataloguing in Publication
Nunn, Bruce, 1962-
59 stories : Nova Scotia's curious connections to the remarkable,
the world-famous and the strange / Bruce Nunn.

ISBN 1-55109-503-3

1. Nova Scotia—History—Anecdotes. I. Title. II. Title:
Fifty-nine stories.

FC2311.8.N84 2004   971.6   C2004-904789-2

Canadä

The Canada Council | Le Conseil des Arts
for the Arts | du Canada

We acknowledge the financial support of the Government of Canada through the Book Publishing Industry Development Program (BPIDP) and the Canada Council for our publishing activities

For Thomas Nunn and Adam Nunn, again.

CONTENTS

INTRODUCTION

(Or, "A *third* book of Nova Scotia stories! How is that possible?")

I thought of writing a prequel. Like they do with serial Hollywood movies these days. You know, the "back story." But, really, not much happened before Mr. Nova Scotia Know-It-All appeared. (That's the cheeky moniker I acquired in my weekly history storytelling gig on Information Morning, on CBC Radio One in Nova Scotia.) Before that…sure, I did radio news reports, researched programs, produced mini-documentaries, and interviewed people about serious newsy stuff. But then, something special happened.

I got lost in the heartland of Nova Scotia: the last best place. The more you become lost in it, the more you find yourself. So many of the stories of the people and the place are timeless wonders—true twists of history that thrill, inspire, and intrigue; that tickle the funny bone or touch the heart. It's been my great luck to explore the magic realm found in this sea-bound place with the archaic name, Nova Scotia.

Is it the age of this old place? The ocean's influence? The character of a people descended from intrepid survivors of the past? I still can't explain it. There's something about this place, something distinct. Its stories reflect that: this is my third volume full of them and, still, the mystery of Nova Scotia's special quality remains.

It's been quite a ride, this story-collecting business. I've been all over: out on ships, on top of lighthouses, down in coal mines, out to islands, and through old tunnels. I've explored historic buildings, haunted houses, dusty cellars, cobwebby attics, clock towers, church spires, ships' holds, movie sets, and a hermit's hovel. I've pored over old photo albums, crumbling diaries, inventor's notes, family Bibles, historic documents, newspaper clippings, microfilm records, internet searches, and encoded carvings. I've talked to fishermen and war vets, coal miners and scientists, musicians and artists, ivy leaguers and farmers, tinkerers and teachers, survivors and rescuers, old folks and little kids. I even talked to myself on one long trip.

And then there's what I call "phone phun time." To a journalist, tracking history means reaching out to sources all over the world via the telephone and e-mail lines. Finding live folks with a memory connection, a family link, or a personal passion for the past—so that history comes alive, today. In this way, I've been in touch with Hollywood producers, Churchill's family, wartime heroes, Disney animators, theoretical physicists, swastika collectors, shipwreck divers, Oscar winners, and waterfall hunters. Not to mention leading experts in brain surgery, comic book history, elephant care, breast cancer breakthroughs, swordfishing, mapmaking, and Moby-Dick. Just to name a few. I've also talked with slavery descendants, barrel makers, pioneer pilots, war nurses, marathon winners, and ghost spotters.

Yes, I've had some exploits. Exploits so eclectic, just listing them makes me sound like Dr. Seuss:

> *I've studied toponymists, theorists, leftists, and goats.*
> *I've researched Nazis, contraltos, inventors, and boats.*
> *Been deep in the woods,*
> *And far out to sea.*
> *I've seen Nova Scotia.*
> *Now can it see me?*

It certainly has seen a lot of me. Perhaps too much. But, I hope you can see Nova Scotia—the heart of Nova Scotia—through reading these stories about its fascinating people and its rich past.

This third collection of Nova Scotia stories, born on the radio, now here in your hand, includes true stories of this province that I personally researched and verified. (This is the third in a trilogy of books that began in 1998 with *History with a Twist. More History with a Twist* followed in 2001.)

Many thanks to all the librarians, archivists, historians, curators, researchers, and regular folks with good, long memories who helped me to see into Nova Scotia's past. Thanks, too, to the crew on board the good ship Information Morning, on CBC Radio. Ahoy Don Connolly! Kudos to all Nova Scotian CBC listeners. It's for you I've been "telling these stories from my mouth" every week for years now. Your continual, warm responses to these true tales have encouraged my work.

Finally, thanks to present-day descendants of George Nunn, the man who began the clan on these shores—with his wife, Frances McKeagney. Their story is part of my story and is included in this book.

Enjoy the read!

M. Bruce Nunn

Bruce Nunn
novascotiaknowitall@yahoo.ca

A FIRST-SINKING SURVIVOR

A boy escapes the first ship sunk on the first day of war

Six decades afterward, in clear, dramatic detail, Don Wilcox remembered surviving the sinking of SS *Athenia*, the first Allied vessel destroyed at sea in World War Two. The Dartmouth man was fourteen then, sailing home to Canada with his mother, Dorothy, after visiting relatives.

It was September 3, 1939, the day Britain declared war on Germany. The long, metal steamship *Athenia* was about 400 kilometres (250 miles) west of Ireland, carrying almost 1400 passengers and crew.

Poland had been invaded just two days before. At about 6:45 that night, fewer than eight hours after the ship heard of the war declaration, German U-boat U30 fired a torpedo into *Athenia*'s hull. The explosion hit near the engine room.

"I was standing right up in the very bow when the torpedo hit," said Don as we talked at his Dartmouth home on a quiet, residential street. "I was almost thrown off my feet!"

"The bow seemed to jump about two feet, then she immediately fell back with this heavy list to port," he said.

Seasick passengers below were blasted from their bunks. Men, women, and children were killed. Cooks were scalded on hot stoves.

The interior went dark.

As throngs of people surged upstairs to the deck, young Don pushed his way against the crowd, downward, to fetch his life jacket. No one was allowed on deck without one.

The *Athenia*, with a single smokestack and a fore and aft mast, listed heavily to port, making the lifeboats on the starboard side too high and inaccessible. The ship was filling with seawater. Darkness was falling.

Back up on deck, Don found his mother. The crowd was abandoning ship from the port side. Women and children were first into the over-crowded lifeboats.

The long, hefty lifeboats were lowered onto heaving swells, ten to twelve feet high, beside the sinking ship. From the slanted side of the vessel, Don and Dorothy had to climb down dangling rope ladders.

"*Athenia* had a list of about fifteen to twenty degrees to port," said Don.

"The rope ladders were hanging in midair and as you went down, you were reaching for rungs with your feet and they were going away from you as you put your weight on them."

Don's mother was ahead of him on the ladder, hanging over a crowded lifeboat that was rising and dropping below her. There was a danger of breaking your leg if you landed in the lifeboat as the swell carried it upward.

"She went down and she got to her place and they told her to stop. When the lifeboat came up on top of a swell they said, "Now let go your hands and jump backwards and we'll catch you!' Everybody had to do it."

She made it. And so did Don. Packed in with almost eighty others, young Don helped to row one of the boat's ten oars. The survivors rowed their boats out about four hundred metres (a quarter mile), formed a semicircle, fired flares into the night sky regularly, and rode the swells. People were cold and seasick. Some shivered in wet night clothes. They waited on the waves, hoping for help, for six miserable hours.

Finally, a ship! Near 3 a.m., *Knute Nelson*, a Norwegian vessel, pulled into view. Survivors were hauled on board but one unfortunate boatload was sucked into the rescue ship's moving propeller; a gruesome way to die.

One hundred and twelve people lost their lives that night. Other ships arrived and survivors were returned to Britain.

Don's worried father, home in Canada, didn't know what happened to his family for days until he saw them in a front page photo amid newspaper coverage of the sinking.

Don's mother was deeply affected by the brush with death.

"She put on a very brave face but I do know that she never really recovered from it. She was always [bothered by] loud and unexpected noises," said Don.

It wasn't until the following spring that they were able to sail again for home, in a convoy of ships.

The convoy was headed for Montreal but three ships peeled away, one with Don and his mom on board. They took a zigzag route, ending up in Halifax Harbour. The pre-planned re-routing was kept secret from the passengers because of the special cargo in their holds.

Like three wise men bearing gifts from afar, the three ships arrived carrying "all the gold from the bank of England."

"They unloaded it in Halifax and we watched it coming up out of the holds on normal wooden pallets," said Don. "Little square boxes just the size of a gold bar for each one," he said.

"The *Duchess of Bedford* was carrying an equal amount, and so was HMS *Revenge*."

The gold had been shipped across the Atlantic for safekeeping in case Hitler successfully invaded England. It would be sent by train to central Canada.

Images of these dramatic wartime events were as sharp in Don's memory on the day we talked as they were over sixty years previously, when he was a scared teen escaping the very first shots fired at sea on the day the world went to war.

SS *ATHENIA*: DEPARTED THE DAY WAR STARTED.

WHY ARE ACADIANS CALLED "ACADIANS"?

The Greek and Mi'kmaw origins of a French place name

You don't need to ride an Acadian Lines bus to Acadia University with a group of Nova Scotian Acadians to wonder where the word Acadia comes from. Old Nova Scotia was once a much larger region called Acadia. Hence, Acadians—the French folk who lived there. But the word is not French. Some say this old land of Evangeline has an ancient Greek connection; others say its origins are aboriginal. Get ready for some multiethnic etymology.

According to Alphonse Deveau, the eighty-something author of fourteen books on Acadian history, the word Acadia—or, as the French say, Acadie—is derived from a suffix found in other native words.

"Mi'kmaq, the language, has quite a few place names with *acadie* in the ending," said Deveau, when I called him at his home in Salmon River. "Shubenacadie and Tracadie, and so on," he explained.

In his book, *Two Beginnings: A Brief Acadian History*, Deveau points out that Passamaquoddy in New Brunswick is listed as Pesmacadie on old maps. He cites other authors who traced the word to a Mi'kmaw term that translates as "campsite" or simply as "place," or even "fertile place."

Bernie Francis, a native linguist at the University College of Cape

Breton, told me that term is the Mi'kmaw suffix e'gati. "It means 'place of' or 'land of,'" said Francis.

"From that we get *Acadie* in French, and that became *Acadia* in English," he said.

Or maybe not. There is also the European explanation. Mr. Deveau described that theory too.

"The first mapmaker of this area used the name Arcadia, a name of a province of ancient Greece," he said, "and the area later became known as the Maritime Provinces."

Just to be clear, theory two has a Greek name being given to a Mi'kmaw land that was settled by the French, then dominated by the British. Got it? I warned you about the etymological ethnicities. And there are more. As it turns out, that mapmaking explorer was an Italian sailing from Spain for the king of France! He was Janus or Giovanni Verrazanus, or Verrazano.

"He was a very well-read and learned individual for the time," said Neil Boucher, the vice president of academics at Université Sainte-Anne in Digby County.

Familiar with Greek mythology, Verrazano named the new land Arcadia in 1524. "It was a place that was a quasi–heaven on earth, a paradise or very idealistic area called *Arcadia* with an *r*," said Boucher. "The beauty of the area or the geography reminded him of what he had read," he said. I did some more checking.

"Arcadia is a province in the central Peloponnesus in Greece," said Dr. Geraldine Thomas, a teacher of Greek and Roman classics at Saint Mary's University in Halifax. "It also becomes a sort of metaphor for the bucolic world," said Thomas, "it's used quite often in both Greek and Latin sources for this idyllic countryside: beautiful, shepherds, sheep, that kind of thing."

Arcadia was such a nice spot, the Greek god Pan used to hang out there with his famous flute.

As for what part of the new land the classically trained explorer Verrazano named Arcadia, it is hard to say. "They are not very sure where he landed," said Boucher, "it's somewhere between Maryland and the Canadian province of Newfoundland."

Somewhere on the eastern seaboard, a new Arcadia was declared. The name stuck and other explorers began using it to refer to the whole wide region, eventually refining it to just what's now called Maritime Canada. Later explorers speaking the French language of course had trouble pronouncing the hard *r* sound in Arcadia; among them, Samuel de Champlain, who sailed our shores long after Verrazano.

"Champlain came on the 1604 expedition almost a hundred years later," said Boucher, "and he continued with the name Acadie, with the *r* dropped."

So from whence hails the word? From the native tongue or Greek culture?

A scholarly history of Acadia by Andrew Hill Clark covers events back to 1760 and sides with the native language link. But it was written thirty-five years ago.

Today, according to Neil Boucher of Université Sainte-Anne, popular wisdom has it that Verrazano's Greek connection is a more likely etymological explanation.

"The Verrazano name [Arcadia] appeared on maps, that's why it was upheld throughout the rest of the 1500s," said Boucher, "and then became the permanent name of the area."

"I would give more credibility to the Verrazano theory," he said, "also because, by 1524, I doubt that you would have much European and Mi'kmaw interaction here in eastern Canada at that time."

Whichever is the word's source, the aboriginal or Greek language, Acadia was described by both as a fine, fertile, idyllic place to live. It still is.

THE AMHERST MYSTERY UNVEILED!

What science said about the alleged possession of Esther Cox

The Great Amherst Mystery is still talked about in whispers 125 years afterward. But I've discovered good reason to doubt Amherst's favourite ghost story.

They say nineteen-year-old Esther Cox, living with her older sister's family at 16 Princess Street in Amherst, was possessed by evil spirits. Well known in Amherst and in other parts of the province, this mysterious ghost story has been handed down, passed along, published, republished, acted out, and retold in countless grade school English reports. Kids love such spookiness. But I think in this province, many children and adults—even some who claim they enjoy these stories "just for the fun"—are still bothered in some corner of their minds or in the pit of their stomachs, by the dark aspects of this strange story. Could it be true?

Well, how does one investigate the facts of a paranormal story, especially one that occurred so many years in the past? First, I sought out Tammy Smith, a mother of two in Amherst and Esther Cox's great-great-grand niece. She believes poor Esther was doomed.

"One night she swelled right up and said she felt like she was going to explode and then she was all of a sudden back to her normal self

HAUNTED HOUSE, HOME OF ESTHER COX.

AMHERST'S MYSTERY HOUSE, OR MYSTERY HOAX?

and was unconscious after that," said Smith. Such details have been handed down over generations.

"Things would move in the room," said Smith. "A knife flew across the room and stabbed her."

Smith is repeating descriptions found in Walter Hubbell's old book *The Great Amherst Mystery*. Hubbell lived with Esther and her family briefly, in 1879. He wrote of furniture mysteriously falling over, fires breaking out spontaneously, objects dropping out of nowhere, and cutlery, umbrellas, and paperweights flying at his head!

"Some would say she was a witch," said Smith of her long dead, distant relative.

"The family, they still don't talk about it a whole lot," said Smith, "maybe because my grandfather didn't want to discuss it."

But in the 1870s, sensational news of the mystery spread through the town, across Canada, to England, and the USA.

"It was really well known," said Charlie Rhindress, a playwright with Live Bait Theatre in New Brunswick who wrote the play *Guilty*, about the mystery. "It was in the *New York Sun* or the *Post*; the quote was: 'In all probability the greatest tale of its kind in this or any age!'" he said from his office in Sackville, NB.

Rhindress also read Hubbell's alleged eye witness accounts.

"They were all in the room and Esther was writhing on the bed," said Rhindress.

"Huge bangs were coming from somewhere," he said, "the doctor was checking her over because she was freaking out. All of a sudden, there was a scraping on the wall," he said, "as if a steel spike was carving into the wall in a scrawl: 'Esther Cox, you are mine to kill!'"

Ewww! It sends shivers down your spine, doesn't it? But so much for the ghost; how about some ghostbusting?

Esther claimed communication with a ghost she called Bob Nickle. Even Hubbell agrees that was a veiled reference to Bob McNeal, the man Esther had feelings for; the same man who betrayed her one rainy night. McNeal threatened Esther with a gun and did so-called unnamed things to her. The rape is hinted at in written accounts. Add to that, Esther was a loner, more homely than her sisters and raised without a mother.

Molested and powerless, with no voice in a harsh male-dominated Victorian era, perhaps young Esther went insane and developed a multiple personality disorder. Maybe her fragile psyche was striking out dramatically and she was staging those stunts as a cry for help.

These explanations are offered in a 1919 report by the American Society for Psychical Research (ASPR), a group of psychologists and scientific researchers in Boston; a sort of Victorian X-Files. (One of its founders, Simon Newcomb, America's leading astronomer and mathematician, was also a Nova Scotian, born in Wallace not far from Amherst.) ASPR assigned their leading psychic researcher, a PhD in divinity who also had training in stage conjuring, to analyze Walter Hubbell's book about the Amherst mystery.

Hubbell's wildly expanded version of events was written from scant original journal notes which Hubbell had jotted while living in Esther's family home in 1879. The psychic researcher from ASPR—a Dr. Prince—compared the book to the journal notes it was supposedly based upon and he found many incongruities. Relying also on interviews with family members, Dr. Prince tore Hubbell's account of the so-called mystery to shreds. He found Hubbell's descriptions were riddled with conflicting information, leaps of judgment, and unscientific, biased conclusions.

I've read a copy of Dr. Prince's 1919 report, available at the public library. It was reprinted verbatim in a book by J. R. Colombo called *Three Nova Scotia Mysteries*. The skeptical Dr. Prince observed that

Esther's own sister admitted she never saw any flying objects take off. She only saw them in the air. Perhaps they were thrown by Esther? He suggests the moving chairs that were reported were perhaps pulled by unseen strings. Esther's bodily swelling could have been symptoms of a medical condition.

Prince also notes that Hubbell, an itinerant actor, took Esther Cox on the road, putting her on stage while he gave paid lectures about her strange "possession." The Amherst mystery helped the actor sell books and make a name for himself.

So is the Great Amherst Mystery based on the antics of a young woman in emotional anguish, coupled with the biased reporting of a dramatic showman out to make a buck? Or, is it a slightly exaggerated but nevertheless first-hand account of inexplicable paranormal events corroborated by the townsfolk?

Rhindress, the playwright, is unsure what to believe. "The fact that the story has lasted 125 years and people are still talking about it, and no one has ever refuted that it happened, makes me think that something strange happened," he said.

What is really fascinating, to me, is that a serious attempt at scientific analysis of the events—albeit years afterwards—was conducted and published and yet most people have only heard the eerie, spooky, ghostly interpretation of the Esther Cox mystery. Some folks just don't like to let the facts get in the way of a good story.

ANNE OF NOVA SCOTIA: THE BLUENOSE OF GREEN GABLES

PEI's famous character, and her creator, started out here!

Anne of Green Gables is really Anne of Blue Nose! The internationally famous literary icon of Prince Edward Island may be known for her trademark red hair but her Nova Scotian roots are showing. Strong Nova Scotian influences and origins abound in the lives of both the Green Gables author and the precocious pigtailed character she created. The proof is there in Lucy Maud Montgomery's journals and in her Anne stories. Montgomery scholars agree.

As a young student, Anne Shirley's creator enrolled in the first year of a BA program at Dalhousie University in Halifax in 1895. She was twenty-one. Lucy Montgomery loved college life in Halifax: the scholarship, football games, campus pranks, opera, church, and new friends. She earned her first money as a professional writer in our citadel city. Her poetry and romantic stories earned her a prize as well as profit from the *Halifax Mail* newspaper.

Alas, freelance writing for newspapers has never been a way to make ends meet. After just one school year, the young writer had to return to PEI, to teach. But by 1901, Maud Montgomery was back in Halifax, this time for her first full-time writing job with the *Halifax Echo* newspaper, in a building on Prince Street. (Now the back half of the Old Triangle tavern; the building that formerly housed Joseph Howe's famous printing press.)

As for Montgomery's fictional Anne, she was actually born in this province. It says so in *Anne of the Island*, written in 1915, some years after *Anne of Green Gables* was published. In it, an older Anne travels off the island to the fictional city of Kingsport to go to Redmond University—that's the city of Halifax and Dalhousie University, Montgomery scholars say.

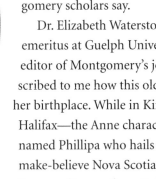

Dr. Elizabeth Waterston, professor emeritus at Guelph University and a co-editor of Montgomery's journals, described to me how this older Anne reveals her birthplace. While in Kingsport—or Halifax—the Anne character meets a girl named Phillipa who hails from another make-believe Nova Scotian town. "Phillipa says, 'I come from Bolingbroke,'

L. M. MONTGOMERY: SHE AND ANNE LOVED HALIFAX.

and Anne says, 'That's where I was born,'" said Dr. Waterston when I reached her by phone.

"So," I asked, "Anne of Green Gables was really...?"

"A Nova Scotian, yes," said Dr. Waterston. "She was born in Nova Scotia."

In fact Anne was adopted from an orphanage in Bolingbroke, which Dr. Waterston thinks might have stood for Windsor.

"Do you really mean it?" asks Philippa in *Anne of the Island*. "Why, that makes you a Bluenose after all!"

(Bluenose is a Nova Scotian's true, traditional nickname. Bluenoser is a recent, ignorant distortion.)

Anne also discovers her true lineage here. "Anne goes to visit Bolingbroke," said Dr. Waterston, "and has a very moving moment when she finds someone who had known her mother and father—they died almost at the time she was born—and has some letters from them."

The famous little island girl discovers a family connection here she didn't expect.

"For the first time, little orphan Anne feels that she can touch the reality of her mother and father and that's in Nova Scotia," said Dr. Waterston. "So it's a very critical moment in the imaginary Anne's life," she said.

The lives of the Green Gables author and her charming heroine intertwine with Halifax as the common focus. Both enjoyed the view from Point Pleasant Park. Many poignant climaxes in the Anne story are set among its pines.

Anne lives on fictional streets near the Old Burial Ground on Barrington Street, and likes exploring that Halifax cemetery. Montgomery lived on Halifax's Church Street, then later on Morris Street, at Barrington, near that cemetery. She also explored the old carved gravestones.

The writer worked in the city less than a year and was forced back to the island again, to be with her suddenly widowed grandmother.

Later, Montgomery married a Presbyterian minister, moved to Ontario, had a family, and lived a mostly unhappy, depressed life. She was a writer out of her element. That's when Montgomery wrote *Anne of the Island*, in which Anne lives the life Montgomery wished she herself had lived: finishing university at Dalhousie and enjoying her youth more in this province.

"She went back to Halifax in imagination in *Anne of the Island*," said Dr. Waterston. "The book expands her real experience in Halifax into four years: what first year was like, what second year was like, what it was like to graduate."

Anne did in Kingsport what Montgomery was unable to do in real life in Halifax.

"She gave her little heroine Anne the college life she didn't have herself," said Dr. Waterston.

Trapped in her Ontario life, Montgomery was looking back fondly on a much brighter period—her time in Nova Scotia—as she crafted the story of Anne's maturing years.

"This is one of the happiest books she wrote," said Dr. Waterston.

THE CHILD SURVIVOR
OF SS *ATLANTIC*

An emotional, modern-day reunion
from the deadly shipwreck of 1873

It's been over 130 years, but this tragic tale of death at sea is still kept alive in the hearts and minds of Nova Scotians—that is the only light in this dark story of disaster. In 2004 I witnessed a twist to this shipwreck saga of 1873. This is a new take on an old story: the sinking of SS *Atlantic*, the greatest single-vessel loss of life prior to *Titanic*.

It happened on April Fools' Day. The steamship *Atlantic* was carrying almost a thousand men, women, and children from Ireland and England, most of them sailing for a new life in America. It was a hybrid vessel; a long, coal-fired steamer with a central funnel and four tall masts rigged for sail. *Atlantic* had crossed the ocean that was its namesake and then steered toward Halifax Harbour to replenish its coal supply. It was supposed to be just a stopover. But *Atlantic* would meet a devastating end here on our coast.

While sailing for the mouth of Halifax Harbour, somehow there was a miscalculation. In the dark of night, *Atlantic* smashed against the large rocks of Marrs Head, off of Marrs Island, which is very near the shores of Lower Prospect and Terence Bay. What followed was horrific. The long steel vessel was stuck upright but was slowly falling over in crashing waves and the frigid wind and rain of April. Mass panic ensued. Many women and children were trapped below in steerage. People clinging to the rigging, freezing in their night clothes, hung on for their lives as long as they could, before succumbing to the bitter cold and dropping into the churning sea. The dreadful scene dragged on through the dark early hours of April 1.

There was a scramble on deck. Some men managed to get a rope secured to a rock on shore. Many men—crew and passengers—had the strength to climb or swim toward shore where rolling breakers threatened to smash their bodies against the rocks. Despite those conditions, many reached the safety of land. But the weaker passengers, the poorer swimmers, and those trapped belowdecks did not survive. That night, 562 people died within a stone's throw of the shore. Only men survived. All the women and all the children perished. All but one, that is.

Remarkably, a twelve-year-old boy named John Hanley—locally known as Hindley—did escape with his life. He was immediately taken in and nurtured by a generous family on Marrs Island.

The boy's amazing survival story has been told in history books and museum displays but it took on a whole new light for me in March 2004, when I arranged a sort of family reunion in his name.

On one side of this special reunion was a living member of young John Hanley's family. I had met Eleanor Fisher Quigley of Alexandria, Virginia, in the late 1990s at the annual Blessing of the Fleet ceremony in Terence Bay. A committee of villagers interested in the *Atlantic*'s story had invited her to the seaside memorial service that honours those lost at sea, including the victims of SS *Atlantic*. John Hanley was her great-granduncle; her great-grandmother's brother.

I was also invited to the ceremony as a thank you for doing an earlier radio story on the *Atlantic* victims buried in the mass grave there. My description of human bones sticking out from the eroding seaside gravesite seemed to catch people's attention. Before long, the village was inundated with local and national television and newspaper reporters, all focused on the travesty of shipwreck victims being slowly reclaimed by the sea. The media coverage worked well for the villagers; soon government funding was offered. A rock barrier was built to protect the mass grave from the ocean's waves. And soon there was an interpretive centre, a seaside gazebo, and a walking trail with descriptive panels and wooden benches for quiet meditation.

Eleanor Quigley told me at the ceremony that she was moved to see that the lost souls of the *Atlantic* were being honoured this way. Especially since they included young John Hanley's brother, and his parents who were Eleanor Quigley's great-great-grandparents. She was so moved, in fact, she stayed in touch with some of the villagers.

Her American father was first to describe to Eleanor their distant relative's near death experience on that Nova Scotian shore in 1873.

"What we understand," said Eleanor, "is, he was among just a handful of people from steerage who managed to get out of the ship."

The boy's narrow escape from steerage was described in old newspapers Eleanor's father looked up. The *Atlantic* sinking was front-page news in the *New York Times*, on April 7, 1873—six days after the accident. The *Times* quotes diary notes made by passenger Richard Reynolds, who was on the deck of the sinking ship:

"Among the last to get out of a porthole," he wrote, "was the little boy, John Hanley, who followed the example of the men in escaping through the porthole.

SS *ATLANTIC*: FROM TRAGEDY TO FAMILY REUNION.

And he cried to me to help him out. I caught him by the hair and lifted him onto the bulwarks beside me. He told me his parents were drowned and asked me to take care of him."

That passenger looked after young John for half an hour then handed the boy over to the ship's captain. The boy was rescued from the ship and taken onto little Marrs Island. A crowd of freezing, dripping men was jammed tightly into the shelter of a small house there. It was the humble home of Sarah Jane O'Reilly and her family. She quickly made large pots of gruel to feed the starving throng. Her sons drilled holes in the wooden floorboards to let all the dripping sea water drain out.

Other villagers were alerted and they flocked to the shipwreck scene to help where they could. Later, after the crowd of wet survivors were dispersed to other houses, Mrs. O'Reilly continued for some time caring for little John Hanley in her island home. She, like him, came from an immigrant Irish family. Eventually, other relatives of the boy arrived to collect him and unite him with his remaining living siblings in New Jersey, where he was raised. Mrs. O'Reilly had grown close to young John but she would never see him again.

However, Eleanor Quigley of Virginia still holds a soft place in her heart for the people of those villages who helped little John all those years ago. That is why I was excited when I received a local call from descendants of Sarah Jane O'Reilly. They became the other half of this special reunion.

John Simpkin, a retired civil servant in Halifax, is Mrs. O'Reilly's great-grandson. I invited him in to the CBC Radio recording studio to talk family history. He earnestly described how he grew up hearing this story from his aunt who remembered Sarah Jane O'Reilly recounting the story first hand:

"[Mrs. O'Reilly] kept the little boy because she thought she could better look after him. He was so afraid because he realized he had lost his parents in the wreck; they had drowned so she kept him for a while."

John and I chatted for a while. His quiet demeanour and gentle, voice did not diminish the pride he has in his great-grandmother's story. In his hands he held a large, oval, framed portrait of her; a family heirloom, which depicts her wearing a jewelled pendant given to her as a reward for the kindnesses she showed the ship's survivors. He told me how that pendant has been treasured for generations, how it's been handed down to a younger relative in Halifax who keeps it still.

So I had talked with distant family members from both sides of this remarkable rescue story, but they had never spoken to each other—and in fact didn't know each other existed. It was obvious what to do next: I had arranged an in-studio conference call so Eleanor Quigley and John Simpkin, two people deeply touched by this history, could meet each other over the phone line. Mr. Simpkin smiled when I told him my plan. We both wore headphones for the three-way conversation.

When I dialled Eleanor in Virginia, she was expecting my call but not my surprise. So I sprang it on her. "Guess who I have with me...?"

She was caught completely and pleasantly off guard but was curious and eager. Did she want to speak with him? Of course she did! The conversation between these two strangers started tentatively but then became a wonderful sharing of details, as if long-lost relatives had finally met.

"John, say hello to Eleanor Quigley," I said.

"Afternoon, Eleanor," he said in a welcoming voice.

"Well, good afternoon, John; how are you?"

She was taken aback. Being polite. Both had so much to say to each other but didn't know where to begin.

"I am fine; how are you?"

"Well, I am doing well," said Eleanor safely, and then she launched into the spirit of the reunion.

"You know, little John Hanley didn't have any direct descendants," she said, "not having been married or anything, but your great-grand-mother and other members of the family made it possible for him to live through what must have been a treacherous, horrible experience on board that ship."

"Yes, indeed it was," said John, "and my great-grandmother just adored this young man. She kept him as long as she could in her little house on Marrs Island."

And then, the story swapping began! I sat back and listened.

"Did you know the story that he had such notoriety that Barnum and Bailey Circus wanted him to tour with the circus?"

"No I didn't know that," said John.

"Luckily, his older sisters with whom he was living there, in Newark, refused to allow permission for that. He had been through quite enough," said Eleanor.

"My great-grandmother," said John, "she lived on Marrs Island with her father and mother and her two boys and from the families of the survivors she received a locket with several pearls and a ruby on it and this locket is engraved, 'From the grateful citizens of Chicago.'"

"Oh wow!"

"And with that locket," said John, "she also received twenty gold sovereigns. She loved that little boy, she really did. My aunt used to spend her summers on the island with my great-grandmother and she has related that various times. But great-grandmother really didn't know if any of his relatives had survived."

"Well, they didn't survive on the *Atlantic*," said Eleanor, "but some had emigrated earlier. So it must have been quite horrible for him to be there when his mother and father and little brother had all died."

"Well it was, but my aunt told me that he was a very strong-willed young man; little boy, really," said John. "But she mothered him and I think that helped him through. I have a portrait in a huge oval frame of my great-grandmother and she is wearing the locket that she received."

"Well, I really hope I get a chance to see that when I am in Terence Bay area in July for the memorial service," said Eleanor, referring to the annual ceremony where she and I had met some years earlier.

"Well, as a matter of fact, I'll come to the service and bring the picture with me," said John, gleefully inspired by the thought.

"Wonderful! Wonderful!" Eleanor was thrilled.

"I'm excited," she said, "and I'm looking forward to seeing you and seeing the picture of your great-grandmother. So thank you so much!"

"Oh, you are entirely welcome," said John, smiling. "I think this is absolutely amazing. This is the last thing that I expected to happen today. Thank you very much."

The two said their goodbyes, and I hung up the phone. John Simpkin was grinning and gently touching the intricate carved edge around his great-grandmother's portrait. I noticed his eyes were a little glassy now, like the curved glass in the old oval frame; a hint of emotion, a feeling of closure perhaps.

On July 27, Eleanor Quigley did come to Terence Bay but John was unable to meet her due to ill health. But his first cousins in Halifax, also direct descendants of Sarah Jane O'Reilly, were eager. So I arranged to bring together the two families linked by tragedy so long ago. The reunion was emotional. Marion Shannon, 82, spoke for the O'Reilly side of the story: "It is history in the making," she said, "after 131 years, our great-grandmother's relatives have met the grand-niece of the little boy that she looked after. It's a wonderful story. He was the only little child that survived."

S. J. O'REILLY NURTURED THE SOLE CHILD SURVIVOR.

Then a copy of Mrs. O'Reilly's old portrait was presented to Eleanor. Her face lit up.

"Oh look at her," she exclaimed. Is this the locket given to her? Gosh I wish I could say hello to her!"

The two women, who had just met, were holding hands. Tears of joy began to flow.

"It's just wonderful," said Marion "I'm so happy, I'm so happy."

"I am very touched that you're here," said Eleanor, tearfully. "It's very sweet. All of you. Thank you all."

NOVA SCOTIA'S ANTI-COMMUNIST ISLAND NATION

A tiny kingdom created by tuna fishermen sparks Soviet anger

It was an island nation, independent and self-proclaimed. A breakaway republic but still part of Nova Scotia! Outer Bald Island was one of the Bald Tusket Islands off Wedgeport: four acres, treeless, flat and plain. You wouldn't have guessed it would become a country, especially not a country that would raise the ire of communist Russia. But it did. In 1949, a wealthy American businessman purchased this island and declared it his own tiny new kingdom: Outer Baldonia. A big Cape Islander fishing boat motored me ten miles offshore to this unassuming island that once drew international attention and controversy. I saw solid stone remains of what the founder, Russell Arundel, had called his castle.

Arundel often fished for sport at the nearby tuna feeding grounds. He bought the island for $750, to keep as a haven for his fellow fishermen from Wedgeport.

On my voyage out I brought Blair Boudreau, a teacher, Wedgeport native, and president of the Wedgeport Sport Tuna Fishing Museum.

He explained that Arundel's Outer Baldonia was to be a political paradise with "no laws, no war; a government where everything was in peace."

Nevertheless, Arundel also arranged for a navy. "He had that in his constitution," said Boudreau.

I asked about the country's currency. "He had the tunar," said Boudreau, "one tunar, one dollar."

So far, so good for a small island nation trying to make a go of it in global politics. But the Principality of Outer Baldonia was a different sort of political haven "where no women would be allowed; where drinking, swearing, lying, cheating, this was all allowed for the local fishermen."

Strange as its national mission statement may sound, Outer Baldonia boasted all the usual trappings of statehood: an official crest, a regal seal of nationhood, documents of state with formal letterhead.

Arundel declared his fellow fisher friends in Wedgeport to be the country's princes—and himself, the Prince of Princes.

Outer Baldonia made itself known to the world. Its consulate was listed in the Washington phone directory. Rand McNally, the map making company, was considering adding Outer Baldonia to its maps.

The Prince of Princes even created his own island country calendar. The year 1949, on Outer Baldonia, was marked as The Year One, OB. Now, if at this point you believe all of the above, you aren't the only one who has been fooled. That's right, this whole thing was Arundel's long-running joke, begun one day when he and his fishing buddies were having a sip in the shelter of the island.

Later, the

"CASTLE" RUINS ON OUTER BALDONIA.

world's media learned of Outer Baldonia and in tongue-in-cheek humour, wrote it up as a newsworthy new nation. It was, alas, just a gag. But not everyone got the joke.

Word of this new country's controversial constitution spread overseas. "Russia was very concerned about this," said Boudreau.

In 1952, a publication of the Russian government called the *Literary Gazette* ran a vehement denunciation of the low morals of this island country that belonged to Nova Scotia. Arundel was accused of turning his people into savages. This voice within Mr. Kruschev's communist Russia was denouncing Outer Baldonia.

Arundel—apparently a rich man with too much time on his hands, and an odd sense of humour—responded in kind. He wrote the Russian Embassy in Washington, threatening severance of diplomatic relations unless amends were forthcoming!

His fake island nation even had ambassadors who played along. One of them was the former mayor of Halifax, Ron Wallace. He was dubbed "ambassador extraordinary, minister plenipotentiary."

Wallace and his sailing fellows in Halifax offered their "services of the Armdale Yacht Club fleet, which became the navy to act in defense of Outer Baldonia."

Wallace still keeps his fancy certificate of ambassadorial appointment. He showed me his extensive Baldonian file during a visit to his south end Halifax home.

He recalls that even some local politicians treated news of the island kingdom seriously. "The minister of tourism," said Wallace, "had a comment in the paper which was quite serious, saying that this didn't represent any threat to the province, that sort of thing."

The former mayor and ambassador laughed and smiled at the memory of Arundel's long-running prank. "It was a flight of fancy and I think he enjoyed it."

Arundel has passed away. His historical hoax faded with time. The island was given to the birds, as a sanctuary. But as late as 1997, the local museum in Wedgeport was still receiving overseas letters—addressed to Prince Arundel—inquiring about information on this fascinating little island country that never was. All hail Outer Baldonia!

OH MY DEER!
DISNEY'S BAMBI WAS
FROM NOVA SCOTIA

How a Shelburne County creature inspired Disney's animators

You've heard of Rudolph, the Rednose; how about Bambi, the Bluenose? It seems Walt Disney animators relied on films and photos of Nova Scotian deer when rendering Bambi and friends for the classic 1942 film.

Our trail to Bambi fame begins with Cecil Griffith, a Shelburne County naturalist known as Laddie, a close friend of the American Loré family who lived across the Clyde River. Dr. Jack Loré was an eighty-year-old surgeon, still practicing at Sisters of Charity Hospital in Buffalo, NY, when I reached him by phone in 2001. He told me about his old pal Laddie's love of wildlife.

"He started to feed a small fawn that came around," said Loré, "because he liked animals."

Soon, the little deer was tamed. By coincidence, Laddie named his tame deer Bimbo, no relation to Bambi.

"Everybody knew about Bimbo, around Shelburne and Barrington," said Dr. Loré.

As a teen summering in Nova Scotia with his father in the 1930s,

Loré filmed Bimbo with his 16-mm camera. He also rigged a still camera so that deer leaping by took their own photographs. "This device I had built," said Loré, "meant a deer would trip a line that tripped a camera shutter and set off the flash."

When his automatic deer-camera photos made it into *Outdoor Life* magazine, his father, Dr. John Loré, Sr., a prominent physician with wealthy and famous patients in Manhattan, proudly posted his son's photos of leaping Nova Scotian deer on his medical office wall. From Shelburne County, Nova Scotia to the Big Apple! Good deer, good!

One day, into that medical office walked 1930s comic actor Jack Oakie, an Oscar nominee who had worked with Charlie Chaplin and appeared in many comedy films of that era. As a comedian, he may have done voices for animated films. Dr. Loré thought he worked for RKO, which was the distribution company for early Disney films like *Bambi*.

Oakie saw the deer photos. "He brought it up that Walt Disney was doing a picture on this animal they were going to call *Bambi* and asked my father if he'd give the photos to him," said Loré.

Loré's father agreed and also offered his son's film of young Bimbo. Oakie "said that would be perfect because then they would be able to actually get how a deer truly runs and walks," said Loré.

The film of the little tamed deer and the still photos of adult deer in mid-leap were sent to the Disney studios for animators to use as models in rendering Bambi and friends. Hard to believe? Well, the eighty-year-old surgeon has proof.

"It's an individual drawing used in the movie *Bambi*," he said, "signed by Walt Disney."

Aha!

"It's framed and it's very nice and stored in my office in Buffalo, New York."

Need more evidence? So did I. I hunted down one of the authors of a 1990 book about the making of the *Bambi* film. The Disney Animation Research Library in California gave me his name: Frank Thomas. The eighty-nine-year-old former supervising animator on Disney's original *Bambi* film was living in Flintridge, California. He confirmed that the animators did rely on such deer films and photos.

"We had several pieces of film that way," said Thomas.

The films were used to "help the background painters get a good view of what the forest would be like and things of that type."

He also remembered using exactly those types of pictures—deer in mid-prance.

"I looked at a couple of things," he recalled. "I wasn't told who shot the footage or where it was taken. I was just interested in the action shots, so editors would drag it out of their vaults for me to look at."

Certainly it seems the Nova Scotia deer film and photos were indeed sent to Disney. And such ideal close-ups would be irresistible to dedicated deer animators. It's likely, even probable, they used our Nova Scotian deer pictures to make Bambi.

"Yes, it is," said the elderly animator, "he [Dr. Loré] is probably telling the truth."

Of course! It must be true! Bambi was a Bluenose!

For further evidence, check the Disney *Bambi* video at your local movie rental store. One copy I rented has a clip of Walt Disney himself at the end of the film, standing next to a stack of grey, circular, metal film cases, which he explains were films of real deer from several sources, which were used by the animators in capturing the woodsy ballet of the bounding Bambi. No doubt our deer, Bimbo, is on one of those films.

As for Bimbo's fate, he was purposely shot by hunters, just like Bambi's mother in the film. Laddie was heartbroken. As for the similar name—Bimbo—it was a coincidence. The Disney deer was named from the book, *Bambi: A Life in the Woods*, written in 1923 by an author in Vienna, Austria.

Laddie Griffith, the naturalist, is buried at Middle Clyde, Shelburne County under this beautiful inscription: "I live by the scent and sounds of spring, the flame of autumn and the tracks of winter."

His faith in nature and in his little tame deer are represented in a stained glass window Dr. Loré had installed last summer at St. Thomas Church in Shelburne.

"It has a deer on the right hand side and on the left hand side it's got the wolf and St. Francis of Assisi in the middle, as a naturalist," Loré said, referring to the legend of the saint's tamed wolf.

"This is to represent Laddie's life and what it was like," said Loré. From Bimbo to Bambi, the little tamed deer lives on in the Disney classic and in the intricate church window.

GOOD DEER. GOOD! SHELBURNE COUNTY SNAPSHOTS INSPIRED BAMBI CREATORS.

A BARREL FULL OF TIME

Old Shelburne factory catered to schooners, pubs, and movie stars

What's that they say about small businesses today? Most go under in the first five years, right? They don't make 'em like they used to. But eighty-seven years ago, a small factory began in Shelburne and—amazingly—they *are* still making them like they used to! Barrels, that is. The same barrel factory is making the same product from the same materials with the same tools, after all this time. It's the oldest operating cooperage in Canada.

My tour amid the wood stacks and sawdust at the rustic cooperage on the edge of Shelburne Harbour brought me back in time.

"I realize there's a long-standing history here and I managed to continue it," said the current owner, Raymond Rhuland. He purchased the barrel-making plant in 1974.

Occasionally Doug Smith, the son of the original owner, stops by to reminisce about the old days and the old ways. He once made barrels alongside his father, Chandley Smith, who started the business in 1917.

"He was producing apple barrels, then moved into barrels for salt fish and the demand was there because we are on the coast and he filled that demand," said Smith, remembering his father's entrepreneurial foresight those many years ago.

Before modern plastic tubs, big wooden barrels on fishing schooners were a necessity. Fishermen poured their daily catch into the chest-high

J. CHANDLEY SMITH, RIGHT: A SUPER COOPER!

barrels made of spruce and oak, shovelled in some salt to maintain freshness, then poured in more fish, more salt, and so on.

"A good many sailing ships came in over the years," said Smith.

"Most of the product he had went to fishermen in Clark's Harbour and Lockeport and seaports along the coast," he said.

Over his fifty-four years on the job, Chandley Smith—Doug's father—turned out probably tens of thousands of wooden barrels. Today, the modern day cooper, Raymond Rhuland, is still producing the heavy duty, round barrels using tools from the past.

"Lots of the equipment is original," said Rhuland, "the old hand-crank windlass and the old barrel heaters are the same from years ago."

He even still uses Chandley Smith's cleverly designed three-in-one rotating saw blade that shapes the barrel, trims its rim, and cuts a groove in the wood, near the top, for the circular lid.

The equipment may be original but the rugged, wooden cooperage building itself only looks old. It is actually quite new. Its dark, shingled exterior includes sharply pointed gables. Inside, the open workshop looks like an unfinished basement, crammed with lumber and machinery.

The windows seem old-fashioned with thick, translucent glass but that's architectural fakery. The building was built in 1994 but in a style meant to fool the eye.

Hollywood moviemakers needed a seventeenth-century look for *The Scarlet Letter*, starring the famous actor, Demi Moore. The 1917 cooperage didn't look old enough so the moviemakers tore it down and built a new older-looking building on the same spot. And they did it fast.

"Thirty days from the day we moved stuff out," said Rhuland, "we were back in, working; pretty slick!"

So it's an eighty-seven-year-old business, in what looks like a four-hundred-year-old building, still serving the same market: fishermen and fish dealers. The staff is smaller though.

"My steady crew went from five or six guys and dwindled to just my wife and I today," said Rhuland.

The husband-and-wife team churns out only about two or three thousand wooden barrels and buckets a year now. Some are still used by fishermen as bait barrels. They also do replica work for museums and breweries. And that old-world look offered by the barrel motif in pub decor has to come from somewhere.

Yes, the markets have shifted and the staff has shrunk, but the Shelburne Cooperage keeps rolling out the barrels in a fashion that would make Chandley Smith proud.

"I remember the last day he was living," said his son, Doug, "he came out and indicated he was not well that morning."

"He went and sat in the garden, and focussed the shop in his eyesight as best he could to appreciate that what had gone on in his life was in front of him," he said. "That was his last day."

How amazed Chandley Smith would be to see his harbourside cooperage still producing barrels in a new building, in a new century, with his old tools!

MR. BELL'S PREDICTION

A little girl's fond memories of the telephone inventor

Yeesh! It's a bloody internet-e-mail-cell-phone-wireless-digital-pager-laptop-computer-voicemail-callscreening kind of world today, isn't it? It's tiring. Hard to believe the beginning of this madness was the simple, wooden, hand-cranked, old-fashioned, party line telephone. After eighty-plus years, Murdena Eldridge's family still has theirs. It's a reminder of the day the telephone inventor himself sat in her grandfather's Cape Breton kitchen and predicted just the sort of modern, high-tech, complex communication I mentioned above.

Murdena, though sightless and living in Halifax's Veteran's Memorial Hospital now, can still see vividly Alexander Graham Bell in her mind's eye. As a little girl in 1921, she sat on the inventor's knee when he visited at her house in St. Anne's, Cape Breton. She listened, fascinated. The grey-bearded Bell was musing aloud about future advances of his telephone invention.

"He said, in the future, you'd be able to see the person that you were speaking to," said Murdena as we sat in her hospital room. Back then, at just five years old, she was a curious little girl.

"I was very interested in this conversation and later, after he [Bell] had gone, the phone rang," she said, "and I went over and took down the receiver but I couldn't see anybody!"

She chuckled at the memory. "I was quite disappointed," she said.

Over four decades later, at the French Pavilion of Expo '67 in

DID A. G. BELL PREDICT THE COMPUTER-CAM?

Montreal, Murdena saw Bell's prediction in reality: a prototype of a viewphone. She could see the person on the other end of the line. She must have smiled that day. And if she were able to see today's world of live, interactive digital computer images from space shuttles, Murdena—and no doubt Bell himself—would be amazed.

The great inventor and Murdena's grandfather used to consult on another Bell experiment: breeding sheep to produce twin lambs instead of just one. Arriving at her farmhouse by horse and carriage from his summer residence in Baddeck, the ingenious and famous Bell also consulted with five-year old Murdena. Sweeping her up on his knee, he would question her.

"I had a pet lamb and he always wanted to know how my pet sheep was doing," she said. "He was a wonderful man; kind, treated you more as an adult than as a child."

Telephones in that day, in rural Cape Breton, were scarce. A switchboard connected callers from the St. Anne's/Baddeck area to Sydney. Murdena remembers that it was the telephone that introduced A. G. Bell to the family of J. D. McCurdy, the man who became his test pilot on Bell's famous first Canadian flight.

As she tells it, on Bell's first day in town, he entered the office of a McCurdy family business, where one of them was struggling with the phone on the wall. It was broken. The bearded visitor opened it up, made a quick adjustment, and said it was fixed! Asked how he learned how to do that, he had to explain that…well…he was Alexander Graham Bell!

Murdena's father, Angus Morrison, perhaps also inspired by those kitchen conversations with Mr. Bell, became the unofficial telephone line repairman for the area once the local pulp company he worked for brought the line in. It wasn't that he was paid to be a lineman for the county. It was just that "nobody else would climb a pole if there was something wrong with the line."

Her dad also repaired local phones with a little inventiveness in the Graham Bell tradition.

"Quite often, with electrical storms, some of the telephones would be damaged by the lightning," said Murdena. "There were quite a few phones around St. Anne's that had pieces of Magic Baking Powder tins as part of them. And they worked very well," she said with a smile.

Her family farmhouse phone was used for seventy-two years, until MT&T put their foot down in 1972! Murdena can still describe even the inside of the old family phone from watching her father make repairs.

When she ran her business, the Tartan Family Restaurant, on the edge of that property, modern-day phone users from abroad were amazed when they went up to the farmhouse to use Murdena's telephone. "I speak into *where*? And hold *what*?!"

The wooden heirloom is now kept on display by Murdena's son Paul Eldridge in Toronto. I called him there on my modern office set. He told me over the long distance line that he still remembers the number of the old party line telephone when he was young: 2-9-7, ring thirteen. Any cool chatroom/cell phone teen reading that today is no doubt asking, "What the…?"

Time flies. Technology leaps. A question occurs to me: Are today's techno-kids as full of real wonder at the power at their fingertips as a young Murdena was, eight decades ago, listening to the marvellous imaginings of Mr. Bell?

BLACK "FIRSTS" IN BLUENOSE COUNTRY

African-Canadians of distinction in Nova Scotia

Sometimes a story I research comes full circle back to me! A new book of black firsts called *Journey: African Canadian History Study Guide* hit my desk just as it hit some school desks in Nova Scotia. It's an encouraging compendium of modern-day and historically notable African-Canadians—many Nova Scotians—who have stood out and made their mark. A couple of the stories in the book were contributed from the Nova Scotia Know-It-All files.

The compiler of these interesting black biographies is Constable Craig Smith, a former Halifax North Branch Library worker, now with the RCMP in Yarmouth. A writer and a Mountie! (He always gets his man-uscript?)

When I opened the book, Noel Johnston's story jumped out at me. In 1948, Johnston was the first black graduate in industrial arts training from the Nova Scotia Teacher's College in Truro, then called the Normal School. Before modern concepts of distance education, Noel Johnston pioneered a new way to teach industrial arts to black students scattered in remote areas.

"He got a milk truck and converted it into what became known as his shopmobile," said Constable Smith when I reached him in Yarmouth. "He had all the equipment, workbenches, and power tools anchored to the floor of it and he moved the shopmobile around from community to community," he said.

A very industrious industrial arts artist!

The author also profiles another Mountie, Inspector Ted Upshaw, who heads up the Cole Harbour RCMP detachment near Dartmouth. From Three Mile Plains, Nova Scotia, Inspector Upshaw is "the highest ranking black law enforcement officer in the country."

"He became the first African-Canadian commissioned officer in the history of the RCMP," said Smith. "He's been at the academy teaching, he's done undercover drug work, he's somebody all of us look up to. He gives us something to strive towards."

The new book also includes this little surprise: a story about a magazine called *Atlantic Advocate*, owned and operated by blacks in Nova Scotia. An amazing accomplishment, given the racial restrictions of that era.

"It was something I had never heard of," said the author.

A Halifax archivist lead him to the 1915 publication. "On the cover of each one it said, 'Devoted to the interests of Coloured people,'" said Smith. It focussed on history, religion, economics and politics. "It sold for a whopping ten cents a month!"

The magazine reached readers across the province and as far as Montreal and Ontario. It folded by 1917. Three of its staff had joined the No. 2 Construction Battalion. The all-black battalion of 605 men, half from Nova Scotia, served the World War One effort not with guns, but with tools and shovels, digging necessary trenches and the like.

It's black heritage worth preserving, although Smith acknowledges the racist attitude of the day that a black soldier could be trusted with a shovel but not with a rifle in his hands.

Several notable African Nova Scotian women are featured in the book, such as Yvonne Atwell of East Preston, the first black woman elected to the Nova Scotia legislature. Deborah Miller-Brown was the first black Nova Scotian to participate at the Olympics, in 1968; a track star.

Then there's Dr. Daurene Lewis, a descendant of Black Loyalists who settled in Annapolis Royal in 1783. And two centuries later, in 1984, she became mayor of that town; the first black female mayor in the country.

All fine firsts!

The story of Thelma Coward-Ince, from Sydney, the first known African-Canadian woman to join the Naval Reserves, was a contribution from my files. So was another all-time favourite of mine.

In June 1999, I was amazed to receive, from the American Museum of Music History, part of the Smithsonian Institution in Washington, a musical score for a song titled "Clara." The Duke Ellington jazz tune was named for Clara Carvery Adams in Halifax. As a teen in the 1960s, she met the legendary Ellington through her mother's cousin, Mildred Dixon, Duke's former girlfriend.

Thirty-some years later, I was thrilled to finally find the archived sheet music to a song Clara herself had never heard. I surprised her in a CBC recording studio with a piano player and Clara's own husband, Bucky Adams, playing the tune on sax. (See my book *More History with a Twist*.)

Duke's mellow music and her tears poured forth. "What a feeling!" said Clara. "I can't believe it. I knew it was there somewhere, it had to be. He was a man of his word," she cried. "This is the first time I seen the music and heard the song."

Her husband had waited many years to play this elusive jazz piece for his wife, Clara. "It was so important to Bucky to get this done... I can't believe it!"

I couldn't believe it either. A special moment in Nova Scotian history was unfolding before my eyes, with all the emotion of it pouring into my microphone. It felt good.

The journey of African-Canadian history in Nova Scotia has been long and at times very rough. But Constable Smith's collection shows that, at certain milestones, there are inspiring men, women, and the occasional magic moment that ease the way.

BLUENOSE VERSUS BLUENOSER: A BATTLE FOR PURITY

The origin and controversy of the Nova Scotian nickname

The origin of the word *Bluenose* is a question that won't sink. It perpetually resurfaces. Why are we Nova Scotians called Bluenoses? Or Bluenosers, as some are wont to say? Though adding the *r* is a source of much fuss and controversy of late. And that's part of the story of our provincial nickname. The question of the word's birth once again buoyantly bobbed up in 2002 with the new issue of Canada's oldest magazine, the restored *Saturday Night*.

This etymological search by *Saturday Night* columnist Joe O'Connor included a call to me. Seems some mischievous museum curator, perhaps tired of this perennial Bluenose question, gave him my number. Guess they thought I know it all or something. Can't imagine why.

Anyway, O'Connor didn't like my answer. Because there isn't one. There are about five, in fact. I listed the traditional options and he set off to research them further. Then he reported back.

"The most entertaining one was in the War of 1812," said O'Connor when he called again.

"Legend has it there was this Nova Scotian privateer vessel that had a cannon on its prow that was painted blue and henceforth they started calling Nova Scotians Bluenoses," he said.

Not true. As he said, that's just legend. There are other more probable explanations for the word.

I consulted Allan Doyle who runs Nova Scotia Tourism's harbourfront information centre in Halifax. He's a passionate and committed chronicler of Nova Scotianna, even in his off-duty hours.

"As far as history is concerned, they often joked about when the French arrived at Port Royal," said Doyle, "the Mi'kmaq used to say the noses of the French turned blue because they were Europeans not used to a lot of snow."

Well, maybe that's true. If the Mi'kmaw word for *blue* were *blue*! But then there's this possible reason too:

"There was the fishing expedition when they'd return with blue mitts and blue noses because Kleenex didn't exist yet," he said.

Aha! The old nose wipe theory. O'Connor's *Saturday Night* piece mentions that one too. But, alas, it doesn't hold water. A curator at the Fisheries Museum in Lunenburg—the birthplace of *Bluenose*—made it abundantly clear to me that in the old days, superstitious fishermen would never set sail with blue-dyed mittens!

"Blue was considered an unlucky colour at sea," said Ralph Getson.

Traditionally, fishermen's mittens were knitted with plain, greyish-white wool. So that theory is wiped out.

What remains is the potato story. Most Bluenose researchers agree, it is most likely that the word came from our blue potatoes, a spud species dating back to the 1700s, sometimes called the MacIntyre potato, known for its blueish hue. These Irish spuds, many shaped like noses, were apparently dubbed "blue nose" potatoes by folks in New England and the Carolinas who took delivery of them from our Nova Scotian schoonermen, who then were painted with the same blue-potato brush. And the name stuck: Bluenoses.

The word was made famous by Thomas Chandler Haliburton, known as the father of American humour. This Nova Scotian author of the famous Sam Slick stories refers to us Nova Scotians throughout his 1837 book, *The Clockmaker*, as Blue Noses, written as two words in his time.

The 1967 *Dictionary of Canadianisms* lists half a dozen old written references to the nickname Blue Nose, or Bluenose, in newspapers and books dated in the 1940s, 1908, 1843 and all the way back to 1785. So, that Nova Scotian word is well established in the historic record.

But—and here's where this word history gets weird—there is no historical record of the word Bluenoser, spelled with an *r*.

"No, there isn't any *r* on the end," said Doyle, adamantly. "I've been fighting that battle lately!"

"It seems in the late twentieth century those who haven't read how 'Bluenose' started, especially with Haliburton, that they've put an *r* on it," said Doyle. He's quite concerned about this etymological abomination. "We are Bluenoses with no *r*, ever!"

So, which came first, the nickname or the schooner? "It refers to the people," said Doyle, "the ship, *Bluenose*, is named after Nova Scotians, Bluenoses."

Doyle thinks the *r* addition is a recent, ignorant usage; a slangish mispronunciation or spelling propagated by local misguided media in the last twenty-five to thirty years. But his recent pleas for historical accuracy have been heard by at least one paper.

"The *Chronicle Herald* admitted the good fight was on," said Doyle.

"They convinced several of their editors to make sure there wasn't an *r* inside the word Bluenose," he said.

Now, official *Herald* policy is to use just *Bluenose*.

In Maritimer-speak, "The *r*'s is out of 'er!," you might say. And yet, "some people still continue to add an *r*, whereas this is a nickname for Nova Scotians, not slang."

So watch out for allegedly patriotic Nova Scotian publications that blatantly violate the historical record of this quintessential Nova Scotian nickname. And think of it whenever you eat an Irish potato.

Bluenose *n.* [see note below]
☛ *The origin of the term* **Bluenose** *is uncertain, as shown by the following quotation:*
1942 DUNCAN *Bluenose* 187: As for the nickname *Bluenose* itself, the last person to tell you why he is so called is a Nova Scotian. Some insist that it comes from the kind of potatoes grown in the province, shaped like a human proboscis and unmistakably blue at the tip. Others believe it to be an outgrowth of the fishing trade, and the naturally resulting color of the noses of fishermen from the North Atlantic winds. Sir Charles G. D. Roberts . . . claims that a famous Nova Scotia privateer in the War of 1812 had a cannon in her bow which was painted bright blue. She made a great deal of money for the province by intercepting United States vessels, and she was called the "blue nose" by those who had occasion to keep out of her way. So the name became associated in the United States with Nova Scotians.
1 a. *Hist.* a Nova Scotian residing in that province before the American Revolution and the subsequent arrival of the Loyalists.
1785 (1902) *Acadiensis* Jan. 65: The Blue-noses, to use a vulgar appelation, who had address sufficient to divide the Loyalists, exerted themselves to the utmost of their power and cunning. **1898** *New Brunswick Mag.* Dec. 30: The soubriquet "Bluenose" . . . originated with the Loyalists of Annapolis county, who applied it to the pre-loyalist inhabitants as a term of "derision" during the bitter struggle to pre-eminence in public affairs between these two sections of the population in the provincial election of 1785.
b. any Nova Scotian (the usual modern sense).
1825 *Novascotian* 4 May 148/2: During the course of the past week I had employed . . . a long blue nose to do the odd jobs. **1959** *Northern Miner* 25 June 26/3: [There were] no fights except among the Irish and "Bluenoses" who fight just anywhere.
c. a New Brunswicker.
1845 BEAVAN *Life in Backwoods N.B.* 2: Of the other original settlers [in New Brunswick], or, as they are particularly termed, "blue noses," they are composed of the refugees and their descendents. . . . **1863** SPEDON *Rambles* 77: To call a New Brunswicker a "Bluenose," he appears neither to feel insulted nor a step lowered in dignity. **1957** *Weekend Mag.* 8 June 55/2: "Break out the hook!"—the first bark of a Bluenose mate [a New Brunswicker] drifted from the water to the shore.

BLUENOSE AT WAR!

Our champion schooner faces a hostile German U-boat

The schooner *Bluenose* at war? It's an odd image. But after the Queen of the North Atlantic's long life as a racing schooner champion, it lived a second life—an exotic and dangerous life—as a commercial vessel during World War Two.

This I learned from Andrew Higgins, son of Tom Higgins, the wealthy adventurer who bought our original *Bluenose* in 1942. Rich and famous, Tom Higgins used to hang out with the likes of Ernest Hemingway, the Duke and Duchess of Windsor, political governors, and corporate giants.

As his son tells the story, Tom Higgins learned there was money to be made shipping to people in the Caribbean starving for food and supplies due to the wartime ship shortage.

Tom Higgins teamed up with another wealthy adventurer, Jesse Spalding III. They formed the West Indies Trading Company and came to Lunenburg to shop for fast schooners to form a fleet. *Bluenose* they knew by its winning reputation. Captain Angus Walters couldn't get government support to keep the ship sailing so he sold it to Higgins and Spalding for about $20,000.

The former race-winner did wartime trade with Mexico, South America, Venezuela, Nicaragua, and other countries, using its new engine power more than sail.

Bluenose shipped about 230,000 coconuts from Honduras to Florida.

The strangest cargo our great schooner shipped during that era was on board when the bold Higgins and Spalding team sailed it to Cuba.

"They put their Cadillac on it and sailed it from Florida to Cuba," said Andrew Higgins when I reached him by phone in Newport Beach, California. The retired police officer has published *World War Two Adventures of Canada's Bluenose.*

"They put it on the *Bluenose* and sailed it over with a tarp on it," he said.

When their wives drove the Caddy into Havana, they were stopped by Cuban police because "they had probably the only car in Cuba with Florida licence plates."

Bluenose was a merchant mariner vessel of sorts, shipping wartime ammunition as well.

"At the time *Bluenose* started the shipping, there was no air cover for ships in the Caribbean or really almost no air cover between Halifax and the Panama Canal and the Allied shipping losses were tremendous," said Higgins.

The author described how *Bluenose* played a vital part in the Allied war effort by transporting dynamite, aviation fuel, and aerial bombs.

"The dynamite," said Higgins, "was then used to build airstrips and military bases all through the Caribbean, Mexico, Central America and the northern part of South America."

For several years, *Bluenose*'s captain and some crew were still Lunenburgers, mixed with Cuban sailors. The Higgins book claims some traders insisted their goods be shipped on *Bluenose*. It was celebrated in many ports on its first visit. Its fame was international. One time, its reputation actually saved the crew's lives.

A hostile German U-boat patrolling shipping routes stopped *Bluenose* for questioning. Hailed on a loudspeaker by the submarine's captain, the schooner crew knew it was a moment of grave danger.

"They said they were the *Bluenose* and that they were fishing, which wasn't a very good lie," said Higgins.

In fact, they were loaded to the gunwales with wartime explosives.

"They had aviation fuel and dynamite on board," said Higgins, "so just a few small arms' fire would have blown the whole ship to pieces!"

But *Bluenose*'s reputation preceded it. "The captain of the German submarine said that if he didn't love that ship he would have blown them up."

The German simply ordered them to return to port right away. Later, Higgins's father and his partner apparently learned that German intelligence was so good "that the German captain *did* know what *Bluenose* had in her cargo hold but he let her go anyway!"

But *Bluenose* wasn't invincible. On January 28, 1946 our champion schooner finally met its demise on a reef off Haiti. It ran out of lives. Or maybe it was put to death. Some say it was no accident. Higgins's father's company had sold *Bluenose* to another trading firm just a year before it sank. A letter from its last skipper, a Captain Berringer, to its first, Angus Walters in Lunenburg, describes its sinking. Berringer reluctantly followed the owners' orders to sail into dangerous waters, on a risky, reefy route, at night, with no cargo to offer a steadying ballast. Were *Bluenose*'s new owners hoping for a healthy insurance claim once it wrecked? It's an age-old nautical ploy. The captain's family thinks he and *Bluenose* were set up.

The author and former cop, Andrew Higgins, writes that there is no hard evidence for that. It's just a family suspicion after a tragic ending.

But think of it! *Bluenose* tacked its way through two amazing lives: as undefeated racing champ and as survivor of wartime service. Not to mention the pride its memory still stirs.

TOM HIGGINS: THE MAN WHO BOUGHT *BLUENOSE*.

BONAVENTURE:
THE MYSTERY OF OUR
LAST AIRCRAFT CARRIER

Beloved but scrapped; did the *Bonnie* really survive?

How do you make an aircraft carrier disappear? That mystery is part of the life story of HMCS *Bonaventure*—known endearingly as *Bonnie* to its former crews. Perhaps the most-loved ship in the Canadian navy, *Bonnie* was Canada's last aircraft carrier. Based in Halifax, the 20,000-tonne vessel accommodated more than a thousand crew. Its demise amid controversy left some sailors and airmen refusing to believe it was gone.

The *Bonnie* served thirteen years through the Cold War's most tense NATO operations, tracking Russian subs and performing peacekeeping duties around the world. It sailed our Canadian contingent to the conflict in Cyprus in 1964. Over two football fields long, HMCS *Bonaventure* tied up in Halifax harbour and was a familiar dockside sight to Haligonians, both civilian and navy.

As a floating base for Canada's Tracker airplanes, *Bonaventure* saw many brave flyers launch their small planes from its heaving bow. Lt. Col. (retired) Chuck Coffen, a former curator of the Shearwater Aviation Museum, lifted off hundreds of times; often at night, in the mid-Atlantic.

"The catapult shot is exciting," said Coffen as we talked near a model of the famed carrier. "It involves running the airplane to full power," he said. "The co-pilot gives a quick salute to the deck officer, who then launches you by dropping a flag, and the guy down in the catapult steam room pushes a button and all of a sudden you are rattling down that catapult stroke with your eyeballs stuck back behind your head somewhere; then you're flying!"

Wow. Dangerous? Oh yes. *Bonaventure* had its share of serious injuries and close calls. One time, a pilot named Field flew off the *Bonnie* during a rough sea. A rogue wave shot up just at the moment of liftoff. The pilot flew through the wall of water, pulled up, circled around, and landed, shaken but unhurt.

In 1969 another pilot, Lt. Jack Flannigan, and his crew were revved up and ready for the slingshot catapult. The "go" signal was given. But something snapped. The catapult lost strength. The plane zoomed straight off the moving ship without enough power to pull up.

"The airplane went in the water and the ship overran the aircraft," said Coffen. The flight crew escaped but Flannigan "was swept under the ship."

"He bounced along under the 701 feet of the bottom of the ship," said Coffen, "and went through the propellers at the stern."

Amazingly, the pilot survived. "The propellers only chopped off one of his legs below the knee; he was very fortunate."

The lucky flyer was plucked from the water instantly by *Bonnie's* circling helicopter and was belowdecks in sick bay within three minutes. He was okay. He continued his flying career as a one-legged pilot.

In 1962, when a plane with seventy-six people on board—military families and children—went down 644 kilometres (400 miles) off Ireland's coast, our *Bonnie* coordinated the rescue. Its helicopter, nicknamed Pedro, made several tricky runs out, snatching up survivors. More than two thirds were saved.

But political controversy can sink even the best public figure. In 1967, *Bonnie* underwent a much-publicized multimillion-dollar refit. Three years later, it was sold for scrap. Political cartoonists had a field day with that flip-flop. Or is it ship-flop?

The official word is that it was towed to Taiwan, its metal sold to Japanese car makers. So, our *Bonnie* lies over the ocean. Or perhaps under the hood of your import.

But, not everyone believes that official line. Rumours of *Bonnie*'s afterlife circulated for decades. Many former crew members have claimed a switcheroo was pulled; that the *Bonnie* was taken to India and renamed *Vikrant*.

Vikrant was a vessel of the same class and same look as *Bonaventure*. Col. John Bremner, the military attaché at the Canadian High Commission in Delhi, is quoted saying he's heard from dozens of people insisting the *Vikrant* was really HMCS *Bonaventure*.

I checked with Pat MacDonald, a Canadian navy Coordinator of Disposals, Sales, Artifacts and Loans in Ottawa. He assured me he would do a search for *Bonaventure*'s bill of sale. He called back apologizing. He couldn't find one in the file. Curious.

John Benson, a worker at the Shearwater Aviation Museum, repeated the story of an old *Bonnie* crewman who had scratched his name into one of *Bonnie*'s metal walls after it was sold for scrap. Later, he was on board the *Vikrant*.

OUR BONNIE, OVER THE OCEAN: LIES?

"He looked in the bunk areas and he found his inscription on board the ship," said Benson. "It leaves you to believe that *Bonnie* may not have hit the scrap heap after all," he mused.

Well, it's anecdotal evidence that may leave wishful veterans of *Bonaventure*'s adventures hopeful, if not believing.

Somehow, the souls of much-loved ships survive. Many in this province of the original schooner *Bluenose* know that. It has been so for centuries.

THE BOSTON CHRISTMAS-TREE CRISIS

How the tradition really started, and the year we messed it up

I t all began about thirteen years ago with a sad-looking Charlie Brown Christmas tree. That's when an event coordinator started coming here from Boston each year to help us choose our annual evergreen gift to his city.

The yearly tree we send is of course our seasonal thank you to our American cousins for the medical help they sent us after the December 1917 Halifax explosion. But the year that we sent an ugly duckling tree to Boston, a rapid replacement had to be zipped down for a quick switch before the big public outdoor tree-lighting gala. Ever since, Ed Jacobs, an event coordinator, has been flying here each year for the tree sponsor company, Prudential Financial. He comes to help choose (or approve) our evergreen gift. And he loves doing it.

"It starts when I come in at the border," said Jacobs as we looked up at one of the tall Nova Scotian trees in the running, a forty-six-foot spruce near Blockhouse on the south shore.

"They asked me if I'm here for business or pleasure and I said, 'Both—I'm here to pick the Boston tree,'" he said in his New England accent. "The customs agent's face lit up," said Jacobs. "She knew that someone comes up every year and I was it."

"The people up here are so wonderful," he said, "everyone knows about the Boston tree."

Jacobs, a big-city lad, has gradually discovered the joys of rural Nova Scotia life, like crawling under electric farmyard fences to view a tall tree.

One year, our Natural Resources helicopter landed Jacobs in a farmer's field to take a look at a privately owned tree they had arranged for him to see. When the farm family came out, this Boston tree picker became part of a heart-warming chain of events. It turned out the family had a young son who was being treated for leukemia.

"Our hearts poured out to him, that they were willing to give up this tree," said Jacobs, "but the boy was crying." Apparently the little lad hadn't seen many people from outside his village, other than physicians.

"He thought we were doctors coming to poke at him again," he said. The boy had to be calmed.

"And once we got through that, we had trouble keeping the tears back but we gave him a ride in the helicopter," said Jacobs.

Jacobs' employers in Boston later brought the boy and his family down to see their very own tree being lighted to the cheers of the Bostonians gathered in the cool night air.

"We brought them up on stage and thanked them for the tree," said Jacobs, "and that's what makes it all worthwhile."

Often the Nova Scotian tree owners are so tickled at their evergreen being picked that they pack their bags for Boston. They want to see their tree fully lit, thrilling a throng of thousands in the big city's streets.

The province pays up to five hundred dollars for a Boston tree but some Nova Scotians donate their spruce, just proud to take part.

This thank-you-to-Boston tree relates to events of eighty-seven years ago but not many people realize that the tradition is only thirty-something. It's a sweet seasonal gesture that was actually born of corporate and government image-crafting back in 1970.

"It's my understanding," said Jacobs, it "was at a dinner meeting with the Prudential Insurance company public relations and marketing guys and with similar people from Nova Scotia."

"They came up with the idea of a tree."

As for why Jacobs began coming here about a decade ago to personally select the spruce: "Don't ask," said Jacobs, laughing. "What happened before that…don't ask."

But I did ask. That's when I learned about the year of the Charlie Brown tree disaster. We're more careful now, though.

"We certainly have to treat this tree with a lot of care," said Ross Pentz, Christmas tree specialist with the Department of Natural Resources. "This tree is actually packaged standing," he said.

Wrapped in place, the huge tree is felled, shipped, erected, and decorated outside Boston's stately Prudential Centre. Then, the dramatic lighting ceremony!

"In the past couple of years 25,000 people have shown up," said Jacobs.

Bostonians are treated to imported Nova Scotian entertainment talent as homegrown as the tree itself.

"It's wonderful," said Jacobs, "we have—what's it called?—a *céilidh*, with the fiddles and dancers."

"The people love it," he said, "it's a great show and they're out there in the cold and it's a great Boston tradition."

In 2001 the white spruce chosen was fifteen and a half metres (fifty feet) tall, from the property of Gerald and Iris Medicraft, of South Alton, Kings County. Its thousand points of light were illuminated on December 1 that year, while Bostonians oohed and ahhed.

What a great Christmas marvel to behold! Although, the man coordinating this cross-border Christmas custom confided to me a little seasonal secret. Turns out, Mr. Jacobs is Jewish!

Merry Christmas, Boston! And Happy Hanukkah too.

A NOVA SCOTIAN TREE HELD CAPTIVE IN BOSTON.

OUR PIONEERING BREAST SURGEON

An Acadian physician broke new ground but stays true to his roots

L ong before the medical community accepted it as the norm, a new surgical treatment for women was pioneered in Canada by a maverick surgeon from Nova Scotia. Today, women fighting breast cancer often choose to remove just the unwanted growth, not the whole breast. It's known as a lumpectomy; much less devastating than the mutilation of mastectomy. The champion of the less invasive surgical choice for women was Dr. Normand Belliveau from beautiful Belliveau Cove, a place he still comes home to each summer, the land of his Nova Scotian roots.

His Acadian ancestors arrived on that Fundy shore as pioneer settlers in 1763. But he arrived on the shores of pioneer medicine in Canada in the 1960s as a junior professor at McGill University and as a surgeon at the Royal Victoria Hospital in Montreal.

In 1969, through his Place Ville Marie Breast Centre in that city, Dr. Belliveau bucked the medical establishment of the day. Now in his seventies, looking back on that time, he told me from his Montreal home that he felt compelled then to offer breast cancer patients a better surgical option.

"The standard, routine mastectomy meant removal of the entire breast and muscle," said Belliveau, his Acadian accent still seeping through. "It was a very traumatic experience for, especially, younger ladies," he said.

Though common today, lumpectomy surgery wasn't formally accepted in Canada until the 1980s.

A Toronto doctor performed a few in the 1950s but harsh peer pressure and professional criticism halted the practice.

Belliveau faced those attacks too. Accused of doing inadequate, sloppy cancer surgery, he stuck by what he had learned overseas.

He and a Dr. Ray Lawson flew to Helsinki, Finland, to learn about lumpectomies being performed there by European doctors.

"Some of the patients they had operated on way back twenty years before were still alive and had their two breasts and were very happy and had not been mutilated," said Dr. Belliveau.

The two Canuck doctors also observed such surgeries in Stockholm, Sweden, and in Marseilles, France. In comparison, Canada seemed to be behind the times.

"We said it's all right to believe in American philosophy but maybe some of these Europeans are not all that dumb either!"

The two doctors brought the European confidence in lumpectomy surgery home with them. Belliveau began performing them in Montreal in the late 1960s. He continued throughout the 1970s and beyond.

"In '69 everybody at McGill was criticizing me," said Belliveau. "If I presented a paper at one of our meetings, one of my colleagues would get up and say 'Dr. Belliveau should be sued for malpractice because this is inadequate surgery,'" he said.

"Of course, I was never sued," he said simply.

He stubbornly kept offering women this European option. "My practice just boomed," he said. "In 1985, I had already done 2,500 lumpectomies and because we were so-called mavericks and off the beaten track, we were invited to lecture all over the world in South America, in Lima, Brazil, Madison, Wisconsin, New York and Rome," he said.

His pride seemed mixed with vindication as we spoke. "We showed slides of two-breasted ladies who had been treated for cancer ten years before!"

He told me he still gets thank-you calls from grateful, healthy lumpectomy patients even now, thirty years later.

Now, to balance those boasts, I checked the facts with Dr. John Keyserlingk who took over that breast centre from Dr. Belliveau. He confirmed that, yes, mastectomy was once the standard. Also, he recently reviewed old pages out of the operating log at Montreal's Royal Vic Hospital. The evidence is there of lumpectomies being performed in the 1970s. He says it's also in the *Canadian Journal of Surgery*.

Dr. Geoff Porter, surgical oncologist at the Queen Elizabeth Health Sciences Centre in Halifax agreed with Dr. Keyserlingk that the lumpectomy wasn't generally accepted until the Milan Trial. That respected clinical trial of lumpectomies finally gave the broad medical community the formal proof they wanted that lumpectomy, with radiation treatment, did the same as mastectomy in fighting cancer cells.

But that revelation came in the mid-1980s. For Dr. Belliveau, the surgery was routine by then.

This Bluenose physician had come a long way to be ahead of his time. He studied at St. Anne's College at Church Point. He was pointed towards medicine by a favourite uncle. It's a family influence, too, that still draws him home each summer to his land near his ancestral homestead. The doctor comes to be near that place where his Acadian roots stretch back two centuries; a place where one type of pioneer meets another.

HALIFAX'S CHINESE PIONEER: WYE ARK LEE

Youngest historian discovers ancestral tragedy and triumph

I n my regular hunt for history, I meet all kinds. Amateur historians abound in this old province. But none so keen, bright, and young as little Thomas Lee. And so confident in his facts! What's more, he represented a slice of Nova Scotia history quite different from the usual. And did so with zeal.

This pint-sized, ten-year-old history hunter was one of many junior researchers invited to Nova Scotia's Government House in Halifax in 2002 for a heritage fair. Amid the usual displays about Nova Scotia mining, fiddling, and fishing, his project really stood out. As did he, the youngest amateur historian I've ever interviewed.

Sharp and polite, this Grade V student at Frank H. MacDonald Elementary School in Sutherlands River, Pictou County, told me his great-grandfather's remarkable survival story.

From a village in China, Wye Ark Lee ended up in Halifax in 1912 after a brief stop in California, where many Chinese once worked the gold mines. Wye Ark Lee's father was dying and arranged for Lee to come to Nova Scotia where a friend would help him settle. Lee didn't speak the language and was unable to get hired so he set up a laundry business on Halifax's Bliss Street.

Almost ninety years afterward, young Thomas Lee traveled to Halifax to interview a granduncle about Wye Ark Lee's challenging life.

"He told stories of how he survived," said Thomas, eager to explain his ancestor's story. "Wye Ark Lee told them how lonely it was and about the hardships of working at the laundry."

The loneliness loomed because Lee's family in China was not allowed to join him.

"In 1923 to 1947 there was an Exclusion Act put to the Chinese and nobody could come to Canada," said Thomas, smartly.

His great-grandfather Wye Ark Lee got into the country before the racist law but it cost him dearly.

"He paid the head tax of $500," said Thomas. "At first it was $100 then it was raised to $200 and so on and it came to $500, which didn't work, so they put down the Exclusion Act," he said.

The smiling lad continued his history lesson cheerily. He showed me that his binder of family research, which looked neat and complete, included a copy of the head tax certificate that had permitted Lee to travel freely back and forth to China. So long as he carried that official proof of payment, he was allowed to come and go.

"They didn't want the Chinese in here because they thought they were dirty and ugly," said Thomas. "But in fact," he said, "they're really nice people!"

He smiled then and shook his head a bit as if recognizing that there's something inherently ridiculous about racism. But then he got to the positive part of his ancestor's story.

"In 1947 they stopped the Exclusion Act and my grandpa came over and so did his wife," he said.

"They must have been really happy after so long and finally meeting back up; just amazing," said Thomas.

Yes amazing, but also tragic. The man had been more than twenty years without his wife and family because of Canadian law. Now that's a piece of heritage that doesn't go down so easy.

Thomas's project book explains that Wye Ark Lee founded the Halifax Chinese Association in the 1930s and it's still in existence. Lee eventually learned English and owned grocery stores, a restaurant, and apartment buildings in Halifax. His is a genuine Nova Scotian immigrant success story.

St. Andrew's United Church on Robie Street houses the Wye Ark Lee library, recognizing the support he gave the church as a thank you for helping him get on his feet.

"The United Church kind of supported Wye Ark and got him through some stuff," said Thomas, "and he became like the mayor of that church."

"He was big to them; he was the first Chinese mayor of the United Church."

Mayor? Close enough. Thomas's family pride was showing.

"He was getting friendly and everybody was with him and there was Chinese associations held at his house; he was a big part of the church and it was just great." This immigrant entrepreneur came a long way. On top of that, according to his beaming great grandson, "he was a fun guy!"

WYE ARK LEE (REAR, LEFT) AND FAMILY: "REALLY NICE PEOPLE!"

WINSTON CHURCHILL'S NOVA SCOTIAN FAMILY

The British prime minister's family tree stretches into our backyard

onsider Sir Winston Churchill. His courageous oratorical inspiration, forever associated with the dark days of war, replays in my audio memory these delicate days. Especially since I've come across the Churchillean family line that spikes straight back to Nova Scotia. A direct-descendant link of us to him. I kid you not. Churchill came from Bluenose blood! It's a firm fact, rigidly researched by genealogy experts abroad.

Yes, he of the famous "fight on the beaches" speech, he of the heroic "we will never surrender", he of the jowly, cigar-smoking visage, the V-for-victory salute; Churchill was a great wartime British prime minister who, many have said, was perfect for that role in that era, as if he came along at just the right time. Well, he lived in that era, at that time, only by the direct genetic contribution of a Nova Scotian woman named Anna Baker. She was Winston Churchill's great-great-grandmother. Some believed her to be aboriginal as well.

In *Jennie: The Life of Lady Randolph Churchill*, Ralph G. Martin describes the dark-haired, high-cheek-boned women of Churchill's mother's—Jennie Jerome's—family. The biographer states, "The family legend was that these features were a result of Indian blood." The

Churchill family believed Anna Baker to be Iroquois.

But newer research, in the last fifteen or so years, has uncovered her true heritage: a non-aboriginal Nova Scotian!

Gary Boyd Roberts, the senior research scholar with the New England Historic Genealogical Society in Boston, the oldest such society in North America, has all the details. Churchill's long lineage, backwards from England through North America, and back overseas again has been more fully charted now.

Mr. Roberts explained that this Nova Scotian, Anna Baker, was Winston Churchill's mother's mother's mother's mother. In other words, his great-great-grandmother. "It's matrilineal," said Roberts, "meaning completely through women."

Baker was born in 1761 in Sackville, Nova Scotia, and raised at least nine years on our soil but "she later moved to New York with a husband named David Wilcox and the guesses were that she might be native American or something else that was exotic."

Even the genealogists followed that family legend for a while. But Nova Scotia wasn't Iroquois country. Yet, she was born here. Alas, it turns out Baker was of traditional New England stock. "What we found was she was the daughter of Joseph Baker and Experience Martin who were perfectly ordinary Yankee immigrants to Nova Scotia of the 1759–60 period," said Roberts. "It was a time when a great many New Englanders were going up there," he said from his office in Boston.

Churchill's great-great-grandmother lived in old Nova Scotia until at least 1770, and returned with her parents to the Boston States.

Seems Anna Baker's family had come up to Nova Scotia from USA for only one generation; just long enough to give us this exciting, direct family line link to the mighty Churchill himself.

However…just one small qualifier: the genealogy is legit but the geography has changed. Sure, Winston Churchill's direct ancestor lived in Sackville, but that Sackville is no longer in Nova Scotia. It's now in New Brunswick. Old Nova Scotia of course once included all of New Brunswick, and parts of Maine. We lost Sackville when New Brunswick became a province in 1784. But Baker and her Churchillean ancestral family had gone south years before that. A minor point! Oh yes, she was born a Nova Scotian, there's no changing that.

Want more? We are ancestrally tied to Churchill on his father's side too. Again, no kidding. Elizabeth Snell, a Halifax-based member of the International Churchill Society explains that lineage link in her book, *The Churchills: Pioneers and Politicians.*

BRITAIN'S BLUE(NOSE)-BLOODED PRIME MINISTER.

The Churchills, once of Yarmouth and of Hantsport (a shipping family) are part of the British prime minister's clan. Here's how: Distant relatives named Churchill arrived in Nova Scotia in 1762, from a pioneer Churchill who had landed in Plymouth, New England, around 1640. And that pioneer had come from Dorchester, England where he was "some kind of cousin" to one of the original Sir Winstons who was himself, a distant, direct ancestor of the World War Two prime minister. Follow me?

Basically, the Churchillean family trail goes back eleven generations in North America, from Nova Scotia to New England, crosses the ocean, then connects up with a Churchill who was several generations back from *the* Winston Churchill! And *that*, I dare say, has got to be "the weakest link!" Nevertheless, it is ours to keep. As is the even shorter, stronger family connection on his mother's side. Dare we say it? His people were from here! This is our special influence on the grand Churchill legacy. Ours to hold and to treasure. We will never surrender!

WHEN P. T. BARNUM CAME TO TOWN

Circus sensations and tragedy in Nova Scotia

"THE MOST MEMORABLE OF MORTAL MARVELS! P. T. BARNUM'S GREAT TRAVELING WORLD'S FAIR!"

The headline hype screams out from the page-long print ad in a summertime edition of Halifax's *Morning Chronicle* of 1876. P. T. Barnum's circus was coming to town!

In true Barnum blarney fashion, the ad attempts to charm and tantalize the public with its message written in old circus-style lettering, a potpourri of fonts. "To my friends in Nova Scotia," it proclaims, "I am positively coming in person, for the first time to visit you with my new and greatest show on earth!"

It's classic circus barker material. But I've also read the old newspaper coverage of the circus arrival and believe it or not, Barnum's ad is not all hyperbole. For Victorian Nova Scotians, his circus wonders really were rare and unexpected spectacles of entertainment.

Barnum himself arrived in Halifax with his massive menagerie and carnival acts on three special circus trains. They did shows in Amherst, Truro, and Halifax. Great throngs lined the streets to see the opening parade. Down Halifax's Hollis Street, the spectacular circus parade flowed along with well groomed horses, a musical band, and colourfully costumed characters. Elephants and camels marched along. Haligonians saw "marvellously small ponies" and the "only living hippopotamus in North America!" I'm not sure why "Roman chariots driven by ladies" was considered an attraction. Strangers flocked to the city. Applause went up from the crowd as the circus attractions rolled by.

It took five hundred men to set up the circus pavilions and tents on the Halifax Common. Under the big top, you would pay 50¢ for the whole circus experience: a snake charmer, musical chimes that "worked by steam," the "great living sea leopard" from the Arctic region—three metres (10 feet) long, 363 kilograms (800 pounds), eating 23 kilograms (50 pounds) of fish per day—and many other attractions. Some, not so politically correct by today's standards.

Admiral Dot, "the California dwarf standing a little over two feet high" was on display. As was Captain Costentenus, described in print as "a Noble Greek Albanian, tattooed from head to foot." Only his ears were left undecorated by swirling patterns and animal designs.

Barnum made big bucks here. His ad boasts of his circus's size: "2,000 dollars a day in salaries!" But Barnum's visit to our capital was costly to our keepers of the crown coffers. There were two daring daylight robberies downtown during the circus parade.

Dr. Patrick O'Neill of the Mount Saint Vincent University drama department pointed me towards old newspaper descriptions of the heists. First, people in the Provincial Building went to the windows of the street front offices to watch the marching menagerie along Hollis Street. During the distraction, the provincial treasurer's private office was broken into. Over $1,200 was stolen. At the same time, the Bank of Nova Scotia, down the street, was also robbed. The *Morning Chronicle* reported that bank clerks briefly closed the bank's doors to watch the passing parade. A man came by, claiming he had accidentally dropped an important paper down the sidewalk grate and had seen it drift into the bank's cellar. He asked to quickly go in and retrieve it.

The bank employee believed him! The brazen robber was allowed in, unaccompanied. He slipped out with $17,000! Barnum was right about that sucker born every minute!

There's no word how well Barnum's circus animals were treated. But forty years earlier, in 1836, tragedy struck another touring menagerie that came to Nova Scotia. It put on shows in Truro, Stewiacke, Musquodoboit, Windsor, and Yarmouth.

The menagerie, circus crew, and other passengers boarded the steamer *The Royal Tar*, heading out of the Bay of Fundy, down to Maine. Heavy winds blew up and the steamer was suddenly in trouble. A fire broke out near the boiler. Everyone had to abandon ship. It was going down in flames. The scene must have been horrendous: a burning ship filled with people and animals.

Unfortunately, there was great panic and loss of life, including most of the creatures brought here to entertain in the small towns of Nova Scotia. It's a sad old piece of the past on record at the Yarmouth County Museum and Yarmouth's Firefighter's Museum. But there's a bright spot in the tale. Mogul the elephant went overboard during the chaos but might have survived. One account has him paddling for shore, his trunk held high above the waves. A museum booklet claims he was found lifeless on the shore. But Ron MacDonald, an experienced newspaperman in Halifax in 1963, writes that the day after the 1836 sinking, a farmer at Penobscot Bay awoke to find a peaceful pachyderm gently grazing in his hayfield. An unlikely nautical phoenix, rising from the flames and the waves to live again? Maybe. And, if so, the largest shipwreck survivor I've ever written about!

(Note: History repeats itself in Nova Scotia. For a more modern story about another circus ship fire and its elephant survivor, see page 77.)

BURIED BENEATH
THE BOOKS

The unusual life and death of Canada's first French novelist

T he body of a Canadian literary pioneer lies beneath the basement
stacks of Halifax's Spring Garden Road Memorial Library. Need me
to say that again? I will. Because I am not making this up. No way.
It was a remarkable discovery for me and means even more to the
Corporation Philippe-Aubert-de-Gaspé, the literary fan club in Quebec
that was searching for the grave of our first French Canadian novelist. Philippe-Joseph Aubert de Gaspé was buried in 1841, after a brief,
tumultuous life and a tragic death in Halifax.

This writer was the bilingual son of an English woman and a
wealthy, aristocratic French landlord in Lower Canada, or Quebec. The
writer was named for his famous father: Philippe-Ignace-François Aubert de Gaspé. His large, literary, famous, French Catholic family lived
in a country manor in Saint Jean Port Joli. His novel—his first and
only—is titled *L'Influence d'un Livre* (*The Influence of a Book*). In fact,
his book still has great influence. Most Acadian and Quebec literature
students study Philippe Aubert de Gaspé. His novel is in all the French
Canadian anthologies.

"It is absolutely well known," said Helene Destrempes, a Quebec-
born teacher of French literature at the University of PEI. "It is always

---

mentioned as the first novel worth being mentioned in French Canadian literature," she said when I phoned to inquire.

Born in 1814, Philippe Aubert de Gaspé the junior was very well
educated. Rebellious and brilliant, he became a newspaper reporter
covering the Legislative Assembly of Lower Canada. One day, a member
of the assembly named O'Callaghan, who owned a competing newspaper accused de Gaspé of dishonest writing. A brawl broke out between
reporter and politician. Monsieur de Gaspé was thrown in jail for a
month. But he later got his revenge on the Quebec House of Assembly
chamber. "When he got out a month later, he planned vengeance," said
Professor Destrempes.

"He threw a very stinking product on the stove that was heating the
legislative chamber and of course everyone had to leave," she said. He
created a stink bomb!

"And that's why there was a warrant for his arrest after that," said
Destrempes.

After making the big stink at the legislature, de Gaspé escaped, fleeing Quebec City to hide out in his father's country mansion. "While
there, that's when he wrote his novel," she said, "which is the first novel
to be published in Quebec."

Philippe Aubert de Gaspé *fils* was in hiding and writing during the
infamous Canadian Rebellion of 1837. His novel was novel. Rather
than reflect the nationalist sentiments of the time, it focussed on individual characters. It's a romantic social history with intertwining plots.
It breaks from tradition, mixing old Canadian oral history with the
modern thought of the day; English legends are also added.

His novel was published but the young writer's life went into a
tailspin. His book was attacked for its English influences. He was still
somewhat on the run and his father, the local sheriff, was thrown in
prison for unpaid debts.

Still in his twenties, de Gaspé *fils* decided to leave Quebec. He eventually emigrated to Nova Scotia, in 1840. "Once he got there, he was
already sick and destitute," said Destrempes. "His father was in prison
1838–41, so he could not help him."

But an old school chum of his father's, Thomas Pyke, helped out. He was connected with the poorhouse in Halifax. Pyke got young de Gaspé a job teaching in the orphanage part of the poorhouse; likely a meagre existence. The poorhouse and orphanage stood on a site that now hosts the Second Cup coffee shop on Halifax's Spring Garden Road, between Queen and Brunswick streets. Young de Gaspé also worked briefly at Halifax's other public house, our provincial legislature. He was again a political reporter. But no stink bombs this time.

P. de Gaspé, fils

DE GASPÉ: OUR CITY LIBRARY IS HIS HEADSTONE.

His time in Nova Scotia was troubled and short. At age twenty-seven, de Gaspé was sick, broke and destitute. After a brief, mysterious illness, he died while at the poorhouse. Records of the only Catholic cemetery of the time, St. Mary's, do not include his name. The only other place a poor, broke, Catholic, poorhouse teacher would likely be buried at that time was the poorhouse cemetery, next to the poorhouse itself on Spring Garden Road. Other de Gaspé researchers agree on that point of logic. It's ninety-nine per cent certain, he's there.

Now for the great irony (a truly "literary" device, in this case): In 1951, Halifax's library was built on the site of that very graveyard where lies our first French Canadian novelist. The Spring Garden Road Memorial library marks the grave site of an innovative Canadian author; a fellow raised to love words, to always have a book in hand.

"His spirit must be reading every day," said Destrempes.

Perhaps so, but shouldn't we acknowledge the final resting place of such a spirit? A brass plaque explaining his significance and burial location would be nice. And that is just what members of the Corporation Philippe-Aubert-de-Gaspé had in mind. The chairman of that group flew to Nova Scotia in 2003 with just such a plaque in hand. He invited me to a breakfast unveiling of the metallic memorial. His plan, supported by Halifax city officials he contacted, was eventually to have the plaque mounted on, in, or near the library building. It would be forever a physical reminder that a great Canadian pioneer novelist rests beneath the books in Halifax.

DONALD DUCK WALKED OUR SHORES

Another curious comic book first with a Nova Scotia twist

What is it with Nova Scotia and its comic book connections? Here's yet another: Donald Duck walked our shores. Now I realize I risk pushing the boundaries of tolerance among my serious, academic, historian friends, but here goes anyway: The very first Donald Duck comic book drawn by Carl Barks, and released in 1942, features cartoon scenery from our very own Bluenose country! I am aware that there is probably no PhD thesis in this, but it is a quirky and cool connection, don't you think? Especially when you consider that, today, that original comic book is a very valuable collector's item. Elsewhere in this book I have written about several other historic comic links to this special province: In Superman #1, published in 1939, the comic book storyline is obviously inspired by the headlines surrounding our infamous Moose River Mine crisis of 1936 (see page 67). Clark Kent poses as a draegerman (a word coined by Nova Scotian coal miners) to rescue mine officials trapped underground. Also: the popular Prince Valiant, the medieval hero still appearing in comic strips, was created in the 1930s by Haligonian Harold Foster (see page 168). I mean, for gosh sakes, the first comic strip version of Tarzan also came from Foster's creative quill! What more claim to comic creation does Nova Scotia need to acquire? Well, there's also the Bambi connection (see page 24).

In "Donald Duck Finds Pirate's Gold," the comic book story is set on pirate ships and in small, salty seaports. Disney's talented artist, Carl Barks, who became a household name in comic book circles, relied on magazine photos to render those nautical scenes. He chose pictures found in the May 1940 edition of *National Geographic.* "There was a large feature in that magazine called 'Salty Nova Scotia,'" said Eric Comeau, a comic artist and senior student at the Nova Scotia College of Art and Design. "The article had a lot of material pertaining to ships and small fishing towns and images of three-masted schooners which provided models for a lot of the images he used," said Comeau.

DONALD DUCK'S 1ST COMIC: SPOT THE NOVA SCOTIAN INFLUENCE!

Disney's Donald was already known on film but Barks was drawing the duck for his first time in comic book pages. All this background is included in a history of the Donald Duck comic book which is the sort of literature Eric Comeau consumes with gusto. It states that the opening panel in the original Donald Duck comic—a scene with a wharf and old wooden fishing boats—is based on a photograph of Sydney harbour. Comeau pointed out that the old inn next to the comic harbour scene—the Bucket O' Blood Inn, no less—is drawn from a picture of a historic Nova Scotian building. "It bears a marked resemblance to [the soldiers' barracks building at] Annapolis Royal which I know for a fact it is based on," said Comeau. The ships at sea and the nautical details are very realistic for a comic about a talking duck. All thanks to the bountiful scenery of our famous sea-bound coast.

One comic panel depicts Donald Duck's nemesis, the evil pirate Black Pete, climbing a gangplank from a wharf up the side of a huge wooden ship. Comeau compared that drawing to one of the images of a Lunenburg ship in the old *National Geographic* magazine.

"It's a shot of the ship looking straight at us, just off to the side and it's a very typical ship that you might have seen in Sydney or any of the Nova Scotia harbours," said Comeau.

"There's a lot of attention to the rigging and the form of the ship; very obviously pulled right from photos of Nova Scotian ships."

I searched out a copy of that old *National Geographic* magazine article for my own comic comparison. It checks out. Donald Duck and his three feathered nephews, Huey, Dewey and Louie, appear to be walking harbourside along Any Dock, Nova Scotia.

Is this vital Nova Scotian heritage or mere trivia? Well, it depends on your (or the artist's) perspective, I suppose.

"It reaffirms to me that Nova Scotia is a pretty neat place, visually," said Comeau, "there's a lot to draw on from here."

His sentiment, and even his pun, I found hard to resist. This is a visually engaging place, which seems to have somehow inspired or spawned more than its fair share of comic book artists.

"It's nice when there's a part of comic book history that's related to Nova Scotia," said Comeau, smiling. "It's great. It's a good feeling. I really like that a lot."

Callum Johnston, long-time owner of Strange Adventures, a busy and successful Halifax comic book business, is equally enthused by our Donald Duck link. The world of comics has been Johnston's love and his life's work.

"I think it's a pretty big deal that the backdrop of the first Donald Duck comic book [by Barks]—a lot of it—came from Nova Scotia," he gushed.

"It's very recognizable when you look at it, and then you find out that it actually is based on photographs from here! There's a sort of a bit of pride, because Carl Barks was one of the pre-eminent cartoonists in the world," said Johnston.

How big *was* Barks?

"If he was allowed [by Disney] to sign his work, he'd be better known than Charles Schultz [Charlie Brown's creator]."

Now, that's saying something! It gives all us Bluenoses something to quack about!

SUPERMAN
THE DRAEGERMAN

Our coal miners inspired makers
of movies, comics, and dictionaries

D igging into the history of coal mine rescue workers, I struck Superman comic books! The connection? It starts with a 1907 photo reprinted in Cape Breton's old Highlander newspaper. John Joe McNeil stands posed with a crew of miners, their underground breathing apparatus in their hands. From the Glace Bay No. 2 mine, they were the first organized crew of draegermen in North America. At least, so says the caption. Checking that claim, I learned much of the draegerman—the interesting word, and the daring job.

Tommy Tighe, a retired coal miner in his seventies, told me he was among a Cape Breton crew of draegermen who searched for miners trapped in the terrible Springhill bump of 1958. The disaster was tremendous. Many miners were dead in the crumbled coal mine but a lucky few were left breathing in the underground devastation. Tighe and his fellow draegermen made their way carefully, courageously, down into that black hell, holding a rope, groping in the dark for bodies.

"We'd keep going down to where the problem was and clear debris and hopefully find some survivors," said Tighe.

DRAEGERMEN OF GLACE BAY NO.2 MINE. 1907

"We'd have four hours and we'd have to return to the fresh air base and another team would go in."

Clearly, being a draegerman is a noble profession; its history and origin are naturally of interest to Nova Scotians who have lived and lost loved ones in the coal mining culture that has thrived in pockets of this province for over a century.

The closed-circuit breathing apparatus that draegermen wore was invented in 1904 in Germany by Alexander B. Drager. But the word *draegerman*, which spread to mine rescue workers across the continent and even crept into pop culture in the 1930s, was invented here; coined by Nova Scotian coal miners.

The oldest published sources of that word, cited in the *Oxford English Dictionary*, offer proof. Katherine Barber, the editor-in-chief with the OED's Canadian edition told me from her office in Toronto that one dictionary source for *draegerman* was from 1936.

"It's just a very short quotation taken from the *Ottawa Journal*," she said. It reads: "One of the Stellarton Draeger crew explained to bystanders..." It is a reference to Nova Scotian mine rescue workers from the mine in Stellarton responding to the infamous mine collapse at the Moose River Mine in 1936. The gold mine's owner, and a doctor who was part owner, were trapped underground with a mine worker (see the full story on page 138). It's significant to the history and etymology of *draegerman* that coverage of those rescue efforts went across the continent on radio.

But the word *draegerman* predates even that event.

"The earliest quotation we have to illustrate this word is from 1918," said Barber, the dictionary editor-in-chief. "It's from a Nova Scotian source, a book by R. Drummond called *Minerals and Mining in Nova Scotia*," she said. "The quotation is: 'Draegermen were soon ready but exploration was somewhat impeded by the jamming of the cage at the bottom of the shaft.'"

So it seems we Nova Scotians were indeed first to use that unique coal-mining word. That's significant. But were we indeed first to have an organized draegerman crew, as the 1907 photo from Cape Breton suggests?

The answer is: maybe. The Glace Bay Miners' Museum, draegerman instructor Joey Doucet (with twenty years teaching at Cape Breton's Phalen Mine), and the archivists at the University College of Cape Breton's Beaton Institute, all point to that same photo as the earliest evidence of the first-ever organized draegerman crew.

But Wes Kenneweg, North American president of the Drager corporate office in Pittsburgh, Pennsylvania, could not confirm that. The Drager office in Germany sent over some old records. Apparently, six pieces of Drager apparatus were sold to a mining company in Butte, Montana, also in 1907!

So who had the first draeger crew? Hard to say. Though, if the Butte miners were just buying the gear and the Glace Bay crew was already posing as an organized team that year, it's likely the Caper crew came first, right?

In any event, the Nova Scotian word, *draegerman*, spread. The Drager corporation began using it. A Warner Bros. movie called *Draegerman Courage* hit theatres in 1937, right after our much-publicized Moose River Mine crisis. It's set in Nova Scotia and is about a mine manager and a doctor getting trapped underground.

The international media coverage of that 1936 Moose River Mine rescue drama inspired the moviemakers. The storyline was perfect film fodder: people trapped in a desperate situation, their wives weeping

**NOVA SCOTIA HISTORY
IN A SUPERMAN COMIC!**

on the surface, rescue workers fighting the clock to free the men below, and two nations listening to events unfold in nervous anticipation. A life-and-death struggle with a happy ending. In Nova Scotia, the truth often makes good fiction! So our mining history and our mining word, draegerman, entered the public domain in a big way, on the big screen. Hurray for Hollywood. But not long after, our word also appeared in the very first edition of the Superman comic book!

At Strange Adventures, a comic book shop in Halifax, the owner, Callum Johnston, showed me a copy of that 1939 comic classic. Here's the comic book's plot: The Blakely mine is unsafe. Miners get hurt. Some miserly mine managers go down underground (again shades of Moose River; mine executives going down for a look-see). Kent—a.k.a. Superman—plans to teach them a lesson.

"Superman surreptitiously collapses part of the mine," said Johnston, a recognized comic book expert. "The managers are all trapped and see the terror and anguish that goes with the work."

"When they've got to dig themselves out, they realize this is just impossible work and all the safety equipment is not working because it wasn't maintained properly," said Johnston. The mean mine managers have a change of heart but they fall unconscious, lacking oxygen in the trapped space. "They see the error of their ways and while they are unconscious, Superman tears down the barrier, permitting miners to enter and rescue the group," said Johnston.

In the comic book, Mr. Blakely yells, "Draegermen! We're saved!" Then, "Hurry, there's likely to be another cave-in any second!" Superman saves the day. But from all I've learned, I'd say the real superhero is the mine rescue worker who risks life and limb while fulfilling the duties of that job title created in Nova Scotia. The real Superman is the draegerman.

A DUMBELL SOLDIER IN A DRESS

Memoirs of a wartime female impersonator: a comedy in two parts

You might say that it takes a real dumbell to find humour in war. In fact that's exactly what the Dumbells were good at. That, and wartime singing too. Born in the muck and mire of France during World War One, the Dumbells were a song and skit troupe of talented Canadian soldiers that kept performing for years, even after the armistice was signed. One of their talented cast was a tall, strapping soldier from Nova Scotia who wore a dress and sang like a woman.

Formed under Capt. Merton Plunkett, the Canadian Army Third Division Concert Party, named the Dumbells after the divisional insignia, boosted morale among our boys in the trenches.

"When they first started, the troupe went to London and France to perform even while they were in the army," said Vesta Mosher, a music teacher in New Glasgow who is researching and collecting Pictou County entertainment history.

"Overseas, the Dumbells went to Scotland and entertained troops in hospitals in England," she said during our chat at her New Glasgow apartment. "They played for the king of Belgium during the war."

The Dumbells left Flanders briefly and toured the Canadian Training depots in England. They were booked into London's Coliseum for two weeks, and performed at other fancy London theatres. Mosher gleaned much of the Dumbells' history from *About Pictonians* by the prolific Pictou County history author, the late James M. Cameron.

THE FAMOUS DUMBELLS

Ross Hamilton was one of the Dumbells' two female impersonators. He was very good at it too. Born in 1872 in Pugwash, Cumberland County, he grew up in New Glasgow. On stage, Hamilton transformed himself into the lovely "Marjorie."

"Even though he was a big, tall, husky guy," said Mosher, "when he appeared on stage in a clinging gown, make-up and a wide-brimmed hat, all the troops gave cheers and whistles and applause."

With his first appearance in front of war-weary soldiers, Hamilton brought the house down.

"Right then and there, he was a star," said Mosher. Talk about courage on the front lines!

Old recordings of Hamilton singing as Marjorie reveal that he altered his baritone voice as radically as his looks. He appeared and sounded convincingly feminine.

Cameron writes of an oft-repeated rumour that one of the senior staff officers was so swayed by Ross Hamilton's costume and feminine presence, he tried to pursue Marjorie—er, Ross—romantically! (See page 74.)

Having trouble believing all this? *The Encyclopaedia of Music in Canada*, and album liner notes by Edward B. Moogk of the Recorded Sound Section of our National Library of Canada, both offer proof.

Ross Hamilton really was a World War One female impersonator from New Glasgow. Go figure.

Hamilton first studied music under Pictou County's once well-known music instructors, William Fife and Mason B. MacKay. He enlisted in the Canadian Field Artillery and later became an ambulance driver in the Medical Corps. With the Dumbells, he often played the role of a nurse administering to a wounded soldier on stage.

Somehow Hamilton contrived his deep voice into a high, formal, operatic sounding contralto/falsetto sound. His trademark on-stage expression was "Hello, my deary" and "he always carried a prop of a telephone and simulated a call to a dreamy soldier in the trenches."

"Even the actresses in London would send him their costumes when he got well-known as Marjorie in the Dumbells," said Mosher.

By 1919 the Dumbells re-formed as a post-war vaudevillian troupe. They performed in revues all over central Canada and did twelve cross-country tours. Their revue called *Biff, Bing, Bang!* was the first Canadian musical revue to appear in New York's famous theatre district.

"They were on Broadway and had all sorts of critics raving," said Mosher.

A twelve-week run at Broadway's Ambassador Theatre ain't that shabby.

"They were internationally famous."

The Great Depression and the talkies were the Dumbells's demise. They folded in 1932. Nova Scotia's female impersonator left the world stage to return to live in villages in Colchester and Cumberland County. He served again during World War Two, performing at Canadian military camps. In 1950, he returned to the home town of his childhood to help arrange the entertainment program for New Glasgow's seventy-fifth anniversary as an incorporated town.

In 1965, at age 93, Ross Hamilton died at Camp Hill, the veterans' hospital in Halifax.

He was a Canadian soldier, a musician, a proud Nova Scotian, and at times...a woman. Such variety in one life! Oh, my deary.

A Fake Female Footnote:
Marjorie Himself Recalls his Lustful Suitors

This just in! After writing the above story, I discovered an audio recording that proves true the rumour that a military officer suffered romantic infatuation for lovely Marjorie, a.k.a. Ross Hamilton. Seems the officer was smitten by his comrade's too-convincing performance as a falsetto female. The taped interview is hilarious.

CBC Radio recorded Hamilton himself at age ninety, in 1962, recalling his amusing wartime stage exploits and their effect on one audience member in particular. Garbed as a gal, performing with the World War One singing troupe, the Dumbells, this Nova Scotian female impersonator began noticing one very enthused fan who kept showing up in the front row.

Hamilton's girlish act, colourful makeup, wig, and feminine costume so convinced the amorous senior officer that Hamilton was accosted backstage by the lovesick soldier; a military man with love in his eyes and lust in his heart!

On the tape stored in the CBC Radio archives in Toronto, Hamilton describes in his ninety-year-old voice how Marjorie sang in the delicate voice of a woman while s/he held a rose in her/his white gloved hand to offer to one of the men in the audience. It was part of the act; a bit of audience involvement.

"One night there was a young officer sitting in the front row," says Hamilton, "and during my song I presented him with this rose."

"I could see that there was really love light in his eyes! I thought he'd know who I was," says Hamilton on the old tape, laughing.

Turns out, the soldier—a man named Allingham—did *not* know! He was infatuated with Marjorie! He came to the Dumbells' concert three times.

"He wrote me a note in the meantime," says Hamilton, "and said he'd love to meet me!"

On the third night, the colonel and the corps commander were due to be in their special viewing boxes in the audience, so Hamilton's buddies convinced him to put on a real show and sing to his amorous admirer sitting, once again, in the front row.

"I told them I would," says Hamilton, "if they would see that he didn't get backstage because if he found out I was a man he'd probably kill me! He was bigger than I was."

After the show, Hamilton was talking with the Dumbells' leader, Capt. Plunkett, when he spotted Allingham waiting for him by the stage door. "I didn't know what to do," says Hamilton.

Still in the long dress, make-up and heels, Hamilton took his captain's arm and walked out looking the other way. He rapidly made his way to Plunkett's tent, to hide out.

"I stayed there until about two in the morning," he says.

Thinking the coast was clear, he left the tent to walk back to the hut where the stage was, to change clothes. He passed a sentry who seemed to know him.

"To see a man walking along in a black evening gown with high heel slippers and gloves on the duckboards at that hour of the morning was a little bit unusual," he says.

When Hamilton got back to the stage, who was there waiting but Allingham, the lovestruck soldier!

"My God, I nearly died! I didn't know what I was going to do," says Hamilton. "I was just petrified."

What could he do? He was alone, late at night, dressed as a woman, and trapped by a senior officer who wanted to get to know him better. Hamilton, made up as Marjorie, decided to keep up the act. In strains of laughter, Hamilton explains on the old recording how Allingham then made his romantic moves on him all those years prior. "He took hold of my hand," says Hamilton, giggling at the old memory, "and the time came when he wanted to kiss me!"

He had to think fast. "I said, 'I have rouge on and there are boys inside waiting for me; if you mess up my face, they'll think there's something wrong.'"

So Marjorie convinced the lusty officer to go around to the front of the theatre to wait while Marjorie went in to change her dress.

"I got in the hut, not a soul there," says Hamilton. "So I just took my dress and my wig and slung it off."

As he changed, he figured out an escape plan. "I had to crawl out of a hole as high as the ceiling and jump down," he says.

He ran to his tent, flopped on the bunk exclaiming to his buddy that Allingham was after him and he barely got away.

Hamilton didn't see Allingham again for a while. The officer had been shipped off to battle, was wounded, and was recovering at a military hospital. But that was the very hospital where Ross Hamilton was to be performing next, as Marjorie!

He stood on stage with his usual rose in hand and there, in the front row, he spotted…Allingham! A persistent bloke, he was. We might call it stalking today. But all's fair in love at war, I suppose.

"I realized someone in the front in a wheelchair stretcher had a face that was familiar," says Hamilton.

"I didn't sing to him, of course; I sang to some of the other fellows." That's when poor Allingham's world came crashing down. An English colonel sitting next to him inadvertently spilled the beans. "And he said, 'That's a bloody fine girl that young chap makes,'" says Hamilton.

So the jig was up. The English colonel told the wounded, though still-smitten, officer Allingham that Marjorie was in fact a "chap"; that there were in fact no women on that stage of Dumbells.

Once the truth had sunk in, Allingham was quickly wheeled out.

"I never saw him again," says Hamilton.

The romance never blossomed. Hamilton as Marjorie had escaped one more advance from yet another war-weary soldier who had been too long without the enjoyment of feminine company.

"That was just one of many," says Hamilton with a laugh.

YARMOUTH'S ELEPHANT REUNION

Long after the circus ship fire, a big survivor is rediscovered

Exotic jungle animals, caged and chained on a burning circus ship, came close to death in June 1963. It's an old and well-known piece of Yarmouth's history. But I've discovered a new and happy twist to it.

The *Fleurus*, a thirty-seven-year-old steamer, roughly fitted out to carry the Al G. Kelly and Miller Bros. Circus, limped into Yarmouth harbour, listing and ramshackle. Its imprisoned menagerie included tigers, llamas, cheetahs, bears, lions, leopards, and elephants.

After a performance in town, the animals were paraded back to the sickly ship and caged and shackled on board again. Suddenly, fire broke out in the engine room. Flames and smoke spread. Dramatic pictures taken by a Yarmouth photographer, the late Bob Brooks, captured the chaos.

"The photos show firefighters and a big crane hauling animals in wooden crates out of the bowels of the ship," said Laura Bradley, an archivist at the Yarmouth County Museum, who was quite taken by this story.

"Sharpshooters were standing by with their guns aimed at the animals in case one were to break loose," she said. "It's a sight that Yarmouth has never forgotten."

It was a memorable scene for the old port town. "The sight of llamas being walked down the wharf," said Bradley, "and these three big elephants munching grass at the side of Water Street, and tigers and performing dogs and all the excitement..."

The ship was destroyed but only two animals were lost, a horse and a llama. The three elephants, shackled in the cramped belowdecks, were brought up through the licking flames. Some heard that the unlucky elephants were later involved in a fatal accident while being trucked back home. A sad ending.

ELEPHANTS IN DANGER IN YARMOUTH

But now we know that it wasn't the end! An internet-surfing friend tipped off the Yarmouth archivist to the website elephants.com, which shows a 325-hectare (800-acre) elephant sanctuary near Nashville, Tennessee. Six old elephants, retired from circuses and zoos, roam freely there. One is named Shirley. Her website biography said she was fifty-four years old, was captured very young in the wild, lived a long circus life, and survived a "ship fire in Nova Scotia." Shirley lives!

Comparing the website photos of Shirley roaming with plenty of friends, food, and freedom with the old picture of her chained in that narrow ship hold, Bradley was immediately touched. It looked like it was her!

"I cried," she told me. "Quite frankly, I cried. I was so moved to know that she had come full circle," said the archivist, "to know that she was once again living freely and able to wander, to swim, graze and have the companionship of other animals and to live out her life the way she had started her life, free."

Bradley tried, but was unable, to contact anyone at the Elephant Sanctuary. She had hoped to confirm that Shirley is the same lucky elephant that wide-eyed Yarmouthians witnessed being pulled from the flames of the burning ship. She wanted to let the sanctuary know that Shirley has a history here in Nova Scotia; that she almost died here but was saved; that she was captured in the brilliant photography of Bob Brooks; that she is remembered by the people of Yarmouth. But the archivist and the sanctuary hadn't connected. Over a year passed.

That's when I came along. The story of the circus-ship fire was what I was after, but this modern-day twist to it was intriguing. I told Laura Bradley I'd like to look into it on her behalf.

Eventually, my phone calls were returned and I was speaking with the director of The Elephant Sanctuary in Tennessee, Carol Buckley. She was happy to hear from me and spilled forth the remarkable events of Shirley the elephant's long and rough life. The animal was abused in circuses for years, then left alone in a zoo pen for two decades, which would have about the same effects on such a smart, social animal as it would on a person.

But Shirley's story finally ends happily at that sanctuary in Tennessee. Rescued from her past life, she was taken to that new home by caring professionals to live out her final days with her peers, other pachyderms also saved or retired from the circus life. The sanctuary director told me I just had to hear about the day Shirley first arrived there. It's a wonderful story that seems to prove the adage that elephants indeed never forget. People at the sanctuary can only describe it as a marvellous elephant reunion.

Shirley met Jenny, a young pachyderm she had known briefly at a circus twenty-three years previous! These intelligent animals actually remembered each other and began trumpeting and caressing each other, communicating with their trunks. Shirley turned sideways, letting her long-lost elephant friend reach out and feel Shirley's old scars.

"Jenny touched all these very large burn marks on Shirley's body," said Buckley, "on the top of her head, her back and on her leg."

"We assumed," said Buckley, "that she received those burn scars during the ship fire [in Nova Scotia]." Buckley had her video camera rolling that day and a *National Geographic* TV producer used her videotape of that reunion in their documentary, *The Urban Elephant*, shown often on television all over the world. But their TV story says little of the Yarmouth circus ship fire.

Neither the sanctuary nor the *National Geographic* documentary producer knew much about that dramatic chapter of Shirley's life.

So the sanctuary director was very excited to learn that archived photos exist of Shirley's rescue from that fire; photos which the documentary producer somehow missed.

"A couple of the *National Geographic* researchers called me and said, 'We can't find any information on Shirley and this fire in Nova Scotia,'" said Buckley.

Well, now they know. But really, a simple phone call would have been all it took. Those dramatic professional photos would have been great fodder for a television documentary on an elephant's life. The producer would have loved them.

"I have a sense she'll be disappointed, because she would have wanted to come to your town and interview some people who might have remembered that incident," said Buckley, from her home in Tennessee.

So, will *National Geographic* come to Nova Scotia someday to do a Part Two?

"I have a sense that there might be a follow-up piece," said Buckley, "because this is rich, this is history, this is important. Shirley was a big portion of the *Urban Elephant* documentary."

She's a big portion of Yarmouth history too. It's nice to know she's still around.

A CIRCUS SHIP RESCUE!

ESTONIAN PICTONIANS

A grateful Nova Scotian reunites
with his post-war Baltic homeland

In 1949, there were Estonians among us in rural Nova Scotia. Their country was first caught in the clutches of wartime Germany and then in the brutal grip of post-war domination by communist Russia. Fleeing that turmoil, a young boy and his family stepped cautiously into a rugged wooden cabin on an isolated farm at Marshdale, Pictou County; their new home. Such as it was. But they were glad to leave the military barracks in northern Germany where they endured difficult years as post-war DPs—displaced persons. New Scotland was their new beginning.

An innovative Pictonian, a school principal named David Wilson, had arranged this new life for the forty DPs. He had a dozen cabins built and stocked with groceries. The Estonians sailed on the *Samaria* to Quebec, then travelled by rail to rural Pictou County. Imagine the culture shock.

"People just didn't know what to expect," said John Soosaar, remembering his arrival here at age eight.

"We got on Pictou County Power Board buses," said Soosaar, now a communications advisor for a provincial government department in Halifax.

"They took us two or three miles up a very muddy road to the Wilson farm in Marshdale," he said. "That's where we settled."

Their arrival was big news. Canadian Press and local newspapers attended the happy welcoming at Wilson's farmhouse.

The wooden cabins on the edge of his land were not as festive; just basic shelters with woodstoves.

"You could see the moon through the boards," said Soosaar with a retrospective laugh. "Many mornings there'd be ice on the wash basin!"

"It was actually kind of a step down from the barracks built to military standards left over from the German military," he said, referring to their previous post-war refuge.

When local cars, filled with curious onlookers, lined the road, the newly arrived Estonians were a little nervous. The uncertainty of Nazi Germany was still fresh in their minds.

"My parents said, 'Don't get too close to those cars, you don't know who's there,'" said Soosaar.

"But, by and large, the Pictonians welcomed us," he said. "It was a good experience that led to many friendships."

The immigrants were skilled craftsmen. They built a workshop where they made handicrafts: metal hunting knives and leather goods. Soosaar's father, Olaf, made intricate wood-inlay pieces. His mother, Gertrude, made knitted products. The local Goodman's store in New Glasgow was their retailer.

But this Estonian settlement didn't last long. Most moved away after a year or two, seeking work and better living conditions.

A few families remained. Vicki Kavala, eighty-one, of Lorne, remembers how hard her first winter was, greeted as she was by rutted muddy roads, snow blackened with coal dust, and lonely, remote farms.

"There were no houses and no people," she said. "It didn't look like Germany or England; even different from Estonia," said Kavala, her homeland accent still present. "Winter is completely different in Estonia than here in Canada."

Nevertheless, she and her husband stuck it out, bought a farm, and stayed.

"We get used to it," she said, "we start farming and we were happy. I like it," she said, "I never moved!"

The Soosaars moved their fixed-up cabin into Lorne Street in New

Glasgow. Olaf took a job with Gordon MacKay's lumber mill. The Soosaars became Estonian Nova Scotians.

However, forty years after landing here, John Soosaar's family immigration story came full circle. In 1991, he returned to his family's Baltic state homeland as a Canadian government translator when Estonia was about to be granted its freedom from the Soviets. A wonderful reunion followed.

He met family members he had never seen; people trapped for decades behind the iron curtain. Together, they visited the grave site of Estonia's original leader.

CABINS OF FREEDOM IN PICTOU COUNTY.

The tide of political history changed while Soosaar was there. His cousin showed up with the Estonian tri-coloured flag under his arm. "He was in tears," said Soosaar. "He said, 'Have you heard the news?'"

Moscow had just officially acknowledged Estonian independence, at last. The two men proudly hung their flag out a window; an act that previously would have been punishable by death.

That afternoon, Soosaar looked back from the deck of a departing ferry to a sight he'll never forget.

"The Estonian flag was flying from all the ships in the harbour for the first time since 1945."

His circle was complete: fifty years after his parents had fled Estonia, forty years since he landed in Pictou County as a wide eyed boy of eight, John Soosaar was back in his family's newly freed home country. He'd come a long way from that crude wooden cabin where the moon shone through the boards in rural Nova Scotia.

A FINE FIDDLING FIRST

A master of Scottish fiddle tunes
makes Canada's pioneering recording

A fiddling first in Canada; first to preserve traditional Scottish music on something called a record—that's the claim to fiddling fame attributed to Colin J. Boyd of Lakevale, Antigonish County. His medleys of Scottish reels, jigs, flings, and strathspeys were recorded on an old style 78 rpm album under the Brunswick record label in Montreal. It was March 18, 1932.

Collie's old-world tunes, heard by the ear but felt by the heart, rise from the warped disc with an ethereal sound; nostalgic, scratchy, and stirring. The feel of ancient Highland tradition seeps through.

The respected Cape Breton fiddler Winnie Chafe claimed that Collie's passionate playing also preserved history. "Pioneers like Colin J. Boyd," she wrote, "through their love and dedication to Scottish music, kept the art alive in Eastern Nova Scotia when it was lost for over a hundred years in the Highlands of Scotland."

Born in 1891, Collie Boyd was immersed in the music of his roots when just a wee lad. His daughter, Mary, a PEI resident who researched and collected her father's fiddle recordings, told me, "At the age of three he became fascinated with his Uncle Hughie MacGillivary's playing and he would get between his legs and look up and watch the bowing and fingering."

His elders would say in Gaelic, "The time will come when that fellow will be a fiddler himself."

The music was in his blood. He spent his life playing toe-tapping barn dances and country *céilidhs*.

And yet, here's a fiddler's twist. While living in Boston as a young man, Collie studied classical violin under two teachers, a Bostonian and one from Paris.

"He would play some of Heifetz pieces," said Mary. "He was often invited to churches in Boston to play "Ave Maria" and pieces like that." From Celtic to classic! Now that's musical range.

In Boston, this violin virtuoso also met his Celtic mentor—another Antigonisher. Dan "The Ridge" MacDonald, formerly of Mabou, a fine Scottish fiddler in his own right, greatly influenced Collie's fiddling style.

Years later, back in Nova Scotia, in the family farmhouse late at night, the sounds of adult voices in the country kitchen downstairs— friends and neighbours together—mingled with the sweet sounds of that Scottish style.

"We went to sleep with the sounds of the fiddle," said Mary. "My mother always accompanied my father as he played. She played the organ or the piano."

Surprisingly, none of the younger Boyds took up the instrument but they carried that sound with them throughout their lives. "It couldn't help but enter your consciousness at a very deep level," she said.

There wasn't much money to make from his music. Sure, during tough times he earned a bit in Ontario mining towns, playing rough halls and saloons. But it was when working as a lineman that Collie gained some fiddling fame.

After a devastating sleet storm on Prince Edward Island in the 1950s, Collie went over to restring electrical lines. He stayed months and ended up playing the fiddle strings several times on the very popular Don Messer national radio broadcast. Messer even made one of Colin Boyd's original tunes famous. It was one Collie had adapted from an old Scottish tune taught to him by Dan the Ridge. Collie J. renamed the lively tune "The Little Burnt Potato."

"It was a very well-known Canadian tune and a lot of people attributed it to Don Messer because he played it a lot."

However, fame by fiddle wasn't Collie's focus. He ran the farm in Antigonish County while playing local events and on the local radio station, CJFX.

Several years ago, Mary Boyd met a man from the far north at a conference down here who told her of the strong fiddling tradition up in his region. He said it started when a northerner came down to Nova Scotia "and he met a man whose last name was Boyd and he taught him how to play the fiddle and he brought it back to the Northwest Territories!" She was fascinated. "It probably was my father," she said.

On August 18, 2000, her father was honoured again with a posthumous induction into the Nova Scotia Country Music Hall of Fame in Liverpool. Of course, the Boyd family proudly attended.

Colin J. Boyd was a pioneer player in our thriving Celtic music continuum. More than that, he simply lived and loved the music.

LAST MAN OUT OF PARIS

A student on the run barely escapes the invading German forces

The Germans were coming. Paris was emptying. Harry D. Smith of Halifax was a young man running for his life.

The twenty-three-old-year French student, a graduate of Dalhousie University, was studying at the famous Sorbonne in Paris in 1939. He arrived there just six months earlier, thinking—as many did—that the war would surely end by Christmas. But, by spring of 1940, hundreds of thousands were fleeing the country. The Paris schools were closing. Radio warnings urged anyone who could leave, to go. Smith knew he had to get out, and fast.

The English Channel ports were falling one by one, so he spent a day getting a visa then bought a train ticket for the west coast of France. Smith's great escape is recounted in a slim volume he published in 1975 called *The Last Canadian Out of Paris*.

Was he the last? He certainly did cut it close.

Smith's widow, Joy Smith, heard him tell this story many times. At her Halifax apartment she told me Harry thought he had a good plan for getting out of France. It was the morning of June 12, 1940, just two days ahead of the German occupation. He left at 5:30 a.m. which he figured would put him ahead of the exodus.

"Well, so did millions of other people," said Joy Smith. "When he got to the underground it was just crowded with people and it took him, he said, two hours to get from the underground to the [train] station," she said.

Smith writes that people fainting in the thick crowd around him had no room to fall down. He had no food, just a bottle of brandy. He carried suitcases packed with his year's notes, his diary, and personal mementoes. He had left his books and clothes behind.

After six hours on the subway, he was kicked in the chest trying to board the crowded train but fought his way on. Heading for St. Nazaire on the west coast, he looked back at a pall of smoke over Paris. The Germans were at the city gate.

Smith rode standing up on the shifting metal floor between two train cars, sharing his brandy with those feeling faint. He recalled that a baby was born during the trip. The train finally arrived at St. Nazaire at midnight. He was eighteen hours on the run by then. And still not safe.

He slept on straw the first night, but had a bit of money for a hotel room the rest of the week as he waited for the ship *Champlain*. But he didn't know that ship had already been sunk—it wasn't coming. Soon, the Germans had taken Paris and moved on to the town of Nantes, just east of St. Nazaire. Police proclamations went up, warning St. Nazaire was next. People were ordered to turn in all firearms and to behave. Smith recorded all this in his diary.

Out of money and with the Germans coming from the east, he had to dash again. He decided he was going to head north, not knowing it was under heavy machine-gun fire. But, before he set out, he caught a lucky break while hanging out at the dockside shipping office.

"The shipping agent comes out," said Joy Smith, "and very rapidly tells him in French there are two British destroyers in the basin."

"'They were there last night,'" she said, mimicking what the agent had told her husband, "'and I don't know if they're still there but if they are, go and go immediately!'"

Fortunately for young Harry Smith, he could grasp most of what the French agent was frantically explaining.

"He told him in French to turn this way, that way and the other way and find the ships in the basin which is what Harry did," she said.

"He took nothing with him. He had nothing but the clothes on his back." So much for his carefully kept diary. It had to be abandoned with everything else.

Smith arrived on the basin dock just in time. "Sure enough, there were two British Tribal Class destroyers," said Joy Smith.

The warships' decks were overflowing. Without his proper papers, Smith couldn't prove he was Canadian except that he called out in English. That ship was his last chance. His escape couldn't have been any closer.

"The British sailor said, 'Get on board; we've put the gang plank down for the third and last time,'" said Joy Smith.

So on board Smith climbed; presumably the last person to board those last-minute evacuation ships.

"I would say so, I would say so," agreed his widow. "And of course there were people behind him, clambering to get on. They were mostly French citizens at that point."

An amazing escape for a young man in a terrible time! Another eighteen-hour trip across the English channel on the ship's open deck brought Harry Smith to Plymouth. Later, he sailed safely back to Halifax on the *Batory*.

His persistence unflagging, Smith served in the war as a naval officer, later earned a PhD, taught French for twenty years in Halifax and was president of King's College in the 1960s. He also became provincial ombudsman for Nova Scotia. A full life indeed, given that it once hung by a thin thread, just out of the Germans' grasp.

A FRENCH OASIS
IN A CELTIC FOREST

A new discovery leads to a touching
family reunion in Pictou's woods

Pictou County is all about kilts, bagpipes, and red-bearded Scots, right? Well, yes, there's a lot of that there. But here's a new discovery: an oasis of rural French culture amid the Pictou Scots of the late 1870s. Even Nova Scotia's premier, John Hamm, has trekked out to the remote remains of the old settlement the French called Raymondville. Now, there are plans to breathe new life into it.

A graphic designer named John Ashton is the document digger on this piece of Pictonian past. About ten families were coaxed here from France to help populate our new nation and to work the county coal mines with the Scot settlers. Given forty hectares (one hundred acres) per family, the French lived between Lorne and Trafalgar, close to where the Pictou, Guysborough, and Halifax Counties' borders meet. It's an isolated spot, deep in the trees.

"There's an old log cabin foundation," said Ashton, "and field stones, carried by French settlers to clear an area to plant crops, and an old well and road way."

He's also found "old pottery and an iron skillet and forks, spoons, and relics that they left behind."

Ashton has collected a story handed down in the family of Elmer McKay, the former Pictou County member of parliament. McKay's ancestors had a mill in the Lorne area.

"Elmer said a story his grandfather told him was that one time Louise Bonnet came in to get the groceries," said Ashton. The sack of supplies was so heavy, some local Lorne boys offered to help.

"One of them tried to put the sack on his back," said Ashton, "and it was too heavy so she grabbed it, put it on her back and carried it back to her settlement." Seems those French settlers were some tough!

Peter McKay, son of Elmer, and Pictou County's present MP, is also keen about Ashton's research. Last fall, Ashton escorted the McKays and Premier Hamm into the woods for a little history lesson about Raymondville.

"The premier climbed down into a couple of the old foundations and was just standing there trying to imagine making a go of it out here."

The premier expressed a hope that, with this discovery, Pictou County would be able to more proudly participate in the big Congrès Mondial Acadien 2004, the international gathering in Nova Scotia of Acadian descendents from all over the world. A local committee began work on preserving and promoting the old French site in the woods.

The Raymondville French had names that are uncommon in our Acadian communities; names such as Bonnet, Hommé, Floret, Oudins, Durand, Mazee, Segretain, and Passieux.

They stayed just three years and were mostly gone by 1880, though a few remained till the 1940s. Descendants of the Hommé family still live in Pictou County. Most of the Raymondville French relocated to labour in the mines of Pennsylvania when life here became unworkable due to declining coal prices, crude living conditions, and religious clashes between the French Catholics and Protestant Scots.

A few years ago, a descendant of the Raymondville Hommé family from Pennsylvania arrived in Pictou County to visit her ancestral homeland. Faye Hommé-Zeigler and her husband, Ken, learned of the settlement through Ashton. He hooked them up with their second cousin, twice removed; Lana MacEachern, who writes for New Glasgow's *Evening News*.

The Pennsylvanian couple travelled to Nova Scotia in the fall of 2001 to walk the land their ancestors had worked. The newspaper journalist, MacEachern, had never before met these distant cousins of hers, Kay and Ken.

"But when she and her husband drove into the driveway that afternoon and got out of their vehicle," said MacEachern, "everyone started to hug each other before we had even been properly introduced."

"It was as if they had always been part of the family," she said. Ashton guided this unlikely family group into the wooded settlement site, as he had done previously with the political entourage.

Reaching Raymondville's remains, the American cousins stopped at an old family home foundation and a weather-worn grave stone; about six people are buried out there. The group grew quiet.

"We stood in a circle and said the Lord's Prayer and a couple of blessings for these departed people," said MacEachern.

"That was pretty emotional; it was a solemn moment standing out in this little clearing out in the woods in the middle of nowhere in Pictou County," she said.

Though distant cousins, the newly united family members felt a special bond during that meaningful moment while they stood over their ancestors' resting place.

"Remembering them," said MacEachern, "it was like a family reunion."

"Some of the family members weren't there in body, but I think they were there in spirit."

SAILING THE SEAMAN'S PSYCHE

The sailor's good-luck/bad-luck practices of old

S elling sailors' superstitions by the sea? Sure! It's not a hard sell. They're fascinating. Quirky good-luck practices once performed at sea tell us much about sailor psychology. Since we live in the historic land of tall ships and salty seafarers, let's unfurl a few examples.

Here's one connected to the Easter tradition. Long ago, sailors who found themselves at sea on Good Friday would anchor off shore to deal with the obvious Christian symbolism on board. The spars and masts of all square-riggers created cross shapes. That was bad luck on a Good Friday. The sailors' superstitious solution was laborious. Down on the windy waterfront, Thom Adams of the Maritime Museum of the Atlantic in Halifax, explained to me how those tall ship crews changed crosses into Xs.

"They would make the spars do a cock-a-bill; put the spars on an angle so they didn't form a cross." That was step one in the Good Friday routine.

"Then they would drape all the lines loose and drape the ship in black canvas around the outside edge of the ship," said Thom. But that's not all.

"They'd drag an effigy of Judas around the decks, then keelhaul that effigy, then hang it from the yardarm."

This is where the hot cross bun comes in. The youngest crew member would have to climb the highest mast with the bun in hand and nail it to the top.

Whew! Sounds like a tiring and impractical practice. "They didn't get a lot of work done on Good Friday," said Thom.

So sailors centuries ago mixed faith with folly. But apparently some customs carried on into recent times.

Way back, a bit of dogwood was always included in the ship's design—as a witch deterrent. Even God-fearing Nova Scotian ship builders have been known to add dogwood to their design, just in case. No need to rock the boat.

Landlubbers' lucky charms didn't always work at sea. If you took a lucky rabbit's foot on board ship, you might be tossed overboard because, at sea, it was bad luck. Witches took the form of rabbits or hares. Sometimes the Christian culture and sailors' superstition were blended together. But other times they simply clashed.

"Clergymen and nuns were hated on board ships," said Thom. "These guys used to sit on the fence a lot. When they were home, they'd go along with what the Christian clergy had to say, but in the old days, the gods ruled the seas, so they had to appease the gods."

Those were the seafarers' gods of good fortune. It wasn't exactly logical but when your life depended on a piece of wood and canvas in a stormy sea, you hedged your bets any way you could.

Early Greek fishermen, for example, believed in the power of the evil eye. That's why figureheads on ships always had to be carved with wide-open eyes. To show no evil was in sight, so to speak.

Before the era of the figurehead, "the Greek fishermen used to paint an eyeball on each side of the bow to offset bad luck," said Thom.

Despite the obvious female qualities of many ships' figureheads, the last thing sailors wanted on board in bygone eras was a "she".

"Especially a red-headed woman," said Thom. Sure, ship captains occasionally took their wives and families to sea with them, but the crews didn't like it. Women were simply bad karma on the male-dominated vessels. That's all I'm going to say about that one.

Let's talk animals. Dogs were unlucky, but black cats on a ship were considered to bring good fortune on board, especially if they wandered on by themselves. Bumblebees were also welcome.

But as for the animal with the cloven hooves of the devil, sailors refused to even speak its name on board a ship.

"P-i-g," said Thom, "You didn't mention the name of that animal on board ship."

"E-g-g. You didn't mention that one either," he said. "It must have been really hard to order bacon and eggs in the morning!"

Well, not too hard. Sailors simply made up words for the ones they couldn't say. The p-i-g was called *the little fellah* or *the turf-rooter*. The e-g-g was called a *roundabout* or *hen fruit*. So your breakfast would be a plate of turf root and hen fruit. Ugh. I guess good luck doesn't have to sound good at sea. Happy sailing.

BEASTS AMID THE BLOOMS

Exotic critters that lived in Halifax's Public Gardens

Your basic ducks, swans, and squirrels are tame fare compared to the wildlife that once chattered and chirped in Halifax's historic Public Gardens. Years ago, an exotic menagerie graced those lush Victorian gardens and I hereby strongly suggest, darn it, that the tiny gardens' zoo-that-once-was be resurrected!

Imagine, behind the black wrought iron fence, among the tall trees, rippling ponds, and breeze-blown blooms: a squirrel monkey playfully performing for passing garden guests, a noisy parrot squawking from its perch, and a colourful peacock spreading its natural regalia for the pleasure of the park bench crowd. This zoological display was all there in the 1950s, along the Summer Street side of the popular city gardens. Picture a rustic enclosure of spruce poles and chicken wire where these critters used to hang out, literally. But the tradition of interesting creatures residing behind the gardens' elaborate gates goes back many years before that.

In the 1870s, there were other unusual animals, no longer seen along the trimmed pathways of Halifax's botanical block at South Park Street and Spring Garden Road. A pair of Newfoundland seals was given to the gardens but one of them didn't last long. The old *Acadian Recorder* newspaper reported that the seals arrived in the month of May, but by July, one was deceased. Perhaps even a Newfoundland seal couldn't survive our cold spring weather.

By the 1880s, a few deer meandered amid the greenery of the Public Gardens. They were removed in 1889 to an area just north of Sackville Street.

I once asked a senior Haligonian, Evelyn Power, of her memories of garden creatures and she recalled a bear of some sort living there. In a cage, one would hope.

Bears are one thing, but how would a monkey endure a Nova Scotian winter? Retired gardener

WHAT CREATURES LURKED BEYOND THE GARDEN GATES?

Buzzy Sullivan told me the monkey wintered under the glass ceiling of the public gardens' big, steamy, leafy hothouse, just across Sackville Street. It was like a jungle in there. But monkeys are sociable creatures. Like us, they don't thrive when alone. So by the 1960s a new home was found for the furry critter. Betty Moore, a member of Friends of the Public Gardens, told me the parrot too was expelled from the gardens. Not for succumbing to the temptation of the apple or anything. No, apparently the squawky bird was keeping guests of the Lord Nelson Hotel, just across South Park Street, awake at night.

Today, pathway perambulators in the gardens can see and feed the white swans in the ponds there without even knowing of their royal lineage. In 1926, George V presented a pair of royal swans (nothing to do with bathroom tissue, as far as I know) as a gift to the gardens. In the 1990s, Royal Dutch Airlines gave another pair of swans to the gardens; perhaps the graceful great-grandswans of the original royal gifts.

"Please stay off the grass" is what the small signs in the Public Gardens warn walkers today. There was a time, however, when a certain animal of the hoofed variety was encouraged to tread on the lawn. Alec Wilson of the Museum of Natural History once told me about an old postcard he's seen that depicts a horse-drawn lawn-mowing device.

"It took three people to mow the grass back at the turn of the century;" said Wilson, "one person to lead the horse, one to guide the lawnmower, and one to carry a bucket in case the horse decided to relieve himself."

Now, there's graphic garden nostalgia! Yuck. Though a one-horse-power lawnmower that fertilizes, waters, and cuts the grass all at once ain't a bad deal. Perhaps we should revert to old times. Which is where I started this story. I say bring back the gardens' menagerie. And the horse-drawn lawnmower too. A greater mix of animals and plants in the gardens would give strollers, sun bathers, and stressed-out city folks on their lunch breaks a much more authentic nature experience in the heart of the concrete jungle. So, why not?

"This area has been a spot for horticulture and wildlife for a very long time," said Wilson.

Today though, plant life has the majority in Halifax's famous gardens. So I suggest it's time to return to a better balance of fauna with the flora in our city's one-block nature reserve. Who's with me?

NUNN ON THE RUN! (OR, HOW I CAME TO BE HERE)

From ship-jumper to lightkeeper; my great-granddad's great story

I've made a living telling other people's stories but this time…it's personal. This is the amusing saga of a young, runaway sailor who jumped ship when he hit our shores, fled for his life, and later became one of Canada's early lighthouse keepers; an award-winning one at that! He is also a man I owe my life to.

This gutsy sailor made his escape in 1856 when a British transport vessel steamed into Sydney harbour, Cape Breton. The story that's been handed down, passed around, recorded, and retold is that he and some other sailors staged a desperate and daring dash from the ship when it moored near a narrow strip of land. That strip is a rocky sandbar that snakes out like a crooked arm, almost a kilometre and a half (a mile) into the harbour. The bar originates from the southern shore of the harbour, so that area is called South Bar. It is just outside of Whitney Pier, before Low Point. As they say in Cape Breton, that's where my people are from, on my father's side. They lived there because that runaway sailor eventually settled there. He was my great-grandfather, George E. Nunn.

Why his steamship stopped at that bar—to let the men dig clams, some say—no one knows. But when he and the others were let off, they

GEORGE AND FRANCES NUNN

made a dash for it. Were they deserters of royal service? Well, that's where the essence of oral history in Nova Scotia is put to the true test. Why they ran and the details of their hiding out and escaping are all elements of a story that is now close to 150 years old. And yet, I have a recorded verbal account from someone very close to the source of this saga.

A South Bar woman named Margaret Doyle MacNeil was recorded on tape by a researcher from the Beaton Institute, the archives at the University College of Cape Breton. Over a cup of tea or two, she recounted all the South Bar history stored in her old memory. That was in 1965. At the time, Mrs. MacNeil was ninety-one years old. She had been born at South Bar in 1874. On the old tape, Mrs. MacNeil says she heard this story as a young girl from a family friend, a Mr. Mulligan. He claimed he had helped George Nunn and the other fugitives during their great escape.

"They had a young officer, Mulligan told me," says Mrs. MacNeil on the archival tape, "and they were sick and tired; they were starvin'!"

In her strong Cape Breton accent, she recounts how the runaway men, just off the ship, "could see all the woods, you know, going back to the lake, and they ran. Eight of them."

Now, in Cape Breton, an island of history-conscious people, a story like this can pass easily from mouth to ear, from family to family, and from generation to generation. I remember my brother Jim telling me about being at a party on the other side of the island when an unrelated Cape Bretoner began telling him about his great-grandfather Nunn's ship-jumping story in more detail than Jim himself had ever heard. People of the island tend to remember and retell old community stories, even if they are not their own, and especially if they get laughs.

Mrs. MacNeil presumed the local Irish of South Bar helped the eight men hide because they were British and fleeing a British vessel. Anything to stick it to the Brits! As she tells the story, the runaways were pursued through the woods by armed men from the ship, chasing them on foot.

Her friend, Mulligan, himself a former ship-jumper, discovered the runaways when his stepdaughter went out to milk the cows and spied the eight men in the woods. They had been hiding all night. Patrick Mullins, the customs officer, was looking for them, and had spread the word to be on the lookout for the strangers. But Mulligan didn't turn them in. He gave the men some water then took them up to the McKay farm at Kilkenny Lake, above the road and up a wooded hill. Phil McKay (pronounced McCoy by some locals) hid them in his barn for eight days and nights. Another local man, Charlie Barrington, said he could steal some of the men away to a coal ship bound for Boston; some would go to nearby Caledonia. He dressed the men in overalls and shirts and spirited them away.

But young George Nunn, a mere seventeen or eighteen at the time, remained in the farmhouse of Phil and Margaret McKay because he had injured himself while on the run. Mrs. MacNeil once lived with the McKay's. As she recalls their story, the young runaway in their house was quite nervous that he would be discovered by his pursuers. You can hear the jovial old lady chuckling out loud as she recounts the funnier bits of the story on the tape.

"Nunn's foot was cut all terrible," she says in her thick brogue, "he couldn't hardly walk and every time the dog would bark, Nunn used to get into a spare bedroom under the bed!" At this point, there's a smattering of laughter from those around the table. "Ohh…he [Mulligan] said he was in a terrible way."

Mrs. MacNeil continues the storytelling. She describes the official British uniforms the fugitives wore when they fled the ship. "The beautiful buttons, you know, and the red coats they ran away in; you think it a sin, they burnt them because they didn't want anything to be seen around."

"Well," says Mrs. MacNeil, "that's how Nunn got here!" Then, the adventure turns to farce. Once his foot was mended and he was able to walk again, the poor young sailor was apparently instructed to wear a disguise whenever he left the safety of the McKay's farmhouse. On the tape, the old storyteller begins giggling and guffawing as she retells this tantalizing tidbit.

"When Nunn got all right and fixed up they got him out and sometimes they'd have old Mrs. McKay's skirt on him, raking hay!"

Laughter all around! From Mrs. MacNeil, from the others within microphone range, and, heck, I laughed too when I heard the tape! Not exactly a proud moment in family history though, huh? Ah well, at least it shows my ancestor, George, was bold and willing enough to try innovative tactics if absolutely necessary. He was a survivor. A survivor in a woman's skirt, but nevertheless, a survivor. The ladies on the tape go into hysterics over that image, however. Through the convulsive laughter, Mrs. MacNeil mentions that J. Clyde Nunn—my father—wanted a copy of the memory tape she was recording. Wouldn't he love to hear that his grandfather wore woman's clothes to hide from his pursuers! Probably not, is my guess.

Credit is due to my siblings though. I polled them to see if it was cool to retell this story on the public airwaves in 2003. No one objected. They saw the humour and, hey, it seems like a great story! But was it also good history?

The bit about the dress could be apocryphal. That's fine. And the part about the desertion from duty I could accept, personally, but it didn't seem to fit, historically. As you may know, I'm a stickler in that area.

First of all, 1856 was too late for press ganging so if young George was serving on his majesty's vessel, he did so willingly. That doesn't explain the red coat he allegedly wore. The redcoats were British army. The only sailors in the British navy who wore short red jackets were the marines. Okay, so maybe he was a young marine who grew tired of the British navy and chose to desert for a new life in this new land.

However, research tells me George had sailed into the Crimean War a few years earlier on board a vessel called the *Kangaroo*. And according to Michael Hargreave Mawson, a Crimean War expert in England, the *Kangaroo* was a private merchant vessel then, not a navy ship. No marines on board. This member of the Crimean War Research Society and author of *Eyewitness in the Crimea*, told me that the *Kangaroo* was used only to transport troops. Well, then maybe George was indeed on board as a member of the British army, not navy.

That could explain the red uniform he was allegedly wearing when, years later, he jumped ship in Sydney harbour. The redcoats are coming! But that theory doesn't hold water either. He clearly was not among any redcoated British troops on board the *Kangaroo* in 1854 because there weren't any. The only troops that ship carried at the time were members of a Highland regiment. I don't know what colour their coats were, but

THE NUNN HOUSE AT SOUTH BAR, CB: A CONVENT OF NUNNS?

George, being born in the village of Wortham, Suffolk County, England, would not have been in a Highland regiment. It doesn't add up.

Maybe the redcoat reference simply crept into the story over the hundred-some years of repeated retellings. It happens. Exaggerated detailing is a common quirk of the oral tradition.

So if it wasn't desertion, why the chase through the trees? Maybe George was just jumping from a private contract, escaping a bad job, or a bad captain, or just a bad few years spent toiling at sea. Whatever he ran from, he certainly ran into a much luckier future. Romance and reward awaited him.

You see, while he was holed up at the McKay farm, probably on a day that he wasn't hiding under the bed or out in his skirt, raking the field, George was introduced to Mrs. McKay's niece, Frances McKeagney. Love blossomed. Within the year, they were married. For the son of an illiterate farm labourer who left home as a teenager to go to sea, it was a lucky break. The girl's uncle was James McKeagney, Cape Breton's first member of parliament. He had land, wealth, and position. So guess who ended up with a large piece of harbourfront farmland and a big, beautiful house just down the shore from the very sand bar where he had jumped ship? Our man, lucky George.

Life was good again. In the big South Bar house, George and Frances raised a whole convent of Nunns. They had a farm, animals, a barn, a root cellar, a big well, a wrap-around veranda, and a gorgeous view of Sydney harbour. George became a pillar of the community; a highly regarded senior resident of South Bar, a distinguished, hard-working gentleman. When a federal population count was conducted, George was the census-taker for the area. And in 1872, when a lighthouse for the harbour was erected out at the tip of the long crooked bar, George was chosen as its first lightkeeper. The fact that his wife's uncle was a federal member of parliament under Prime Minister John A. Macdonald at the time and that, with Canada's recent confederation, lighthouses had become a federal responsibility...these facts probably had almost nothing to do with lucky George landing the lightkeeper's job at an enviable $200 a year.

For forty years, George Nunn prospered while tending that light at the end of the same sandspit onto which he had jumped ship as a poor, desperate young sailor on the run. What goes around, comes around. But it wasn't exactly a life of leisure. The open-flame lantern with the curved silver reflector behind it, up in the light tower, needed attention. The wick needed trimming so it wouldn't smoke. The lamp needed constant refuelling. My old aunt, Frances Nunn, a Sydney schoolteacher who often visited the South Bar homestead, once described to me George's life as a lightkeeper there.

"Grandfather was never home," she said, "because he was always in the lighthouse, you know?"

"He'd come home, he'd work all day on the farm but you know he had his bedroom and everything was in the lighthouse," she said. "There was a kitchen and a bedroom and I think a little sitting room; it was like a little house, the lighthouse."

The light was his home away from home. For four decades, he hauled cans of oil or kerosene up three flights of steps to fuel the burning lamp. He did that work until he was seventy-four years old. In February 1913, at a public ceremony in South Bar, George Nunn's lightkeeping longevity was formally acknowledged and celebrated when he was awarded with a long-service medal from his king. Surrounded by the mayor, the local member of parliament, sea captains, neighbours, and four generations of family, the retiring lightkeeper was feted with speeches and a round of three cheers. The occasion was reported in the local newspaper, including the response from George Nunn, keeper of the Sydney Harbour Light. Funny, it didn't sound like the response of a deserter:

"Gentleman, I thank you very sincerely for the honour you would do me in assembling here for the presentation of this medal, awarded by our gracious sovereign for forty years of service under three rulers…In accepting this mark of approval of my feeble services for the public benefit and for the welfare of my family, I feel that I in turn owe a deep dept of gratitude to Almighty God, the King of Kings, who during all these years blessed me with health and strength needed to fulfil my duty."

A KING'S MEDAL FOR KEEPING A LIGHT.

That was my father's father's father. Whatever the details of how George Nunn landed here in Nova Scotia, I'm glad that he did.

NOVA SCOTIA'S HARLEQUIN ROMANCE

Writing our provincial past into the lusty pages of pocket novels

---

I've got five sisters, so I know what a Harlequin Romance is. I grew up seeing those ubiquitous passionate paperbacks with the romantic cover couples: she of the bountiful bosom, he of the manly mane and bared chest. Yup, I've seen 'em. But I never thought I'd see one set in eighteenth-century colonial Nova Scotia.

Julianne MacLean is a young romance writer in Bedford who has published a historical Harlequin melodrama based in our own back-

yard. People of many countries and languages will be reading of our provincial geography and history, circa 1775. I think that's neat.

MacLean has published other Harlequins—including *Prairie Bride* and *The Marshal and Mrs. O'Malley*— both set in Kansas, though she's never been. The graduate of King's and Acadia universities began writing romantically about six years ago while working as a financial auditor with the auditor general's office in Ottawa. As romantic as I am sure Ottawa is, what with the strange bedfellows of politics and all, MacLean returned here to write of a place with true passion.

"I just looked around me," she said, "I love Nova Scotia; it's a beautiful province and it's very romantic."

Her romantic plot idea was inspired by a visit to a conference on the immigration of Yorkshiremen, of all things.

"They had come over during the 1700s," said MacLean, her rough draft in hand as we talked at her dining room table. They settled along the Tantramar marsh area of New Brunswick, in Amherst, and along the modern provincial border. Back then, it was all Nova Scotia, including what is now called New Brunswick.

The Yorkshiremen were coaxed here from England to set up farms along the dykelands left by the expelled Acadians.

The novel's title is *Adam's Promise*. Its lead character is Adam Coates, an actual name of a Yorkshire settler living in Amherst in the 1770s. He's the "man who sends for the sweetheart of his youth and he gets the wrong sister."

"This was a perfect setting because he was in Nova Scotia and he would have written home to Yorkshire, and it would have taken six weeks at least by boat for the real bride to get here—so there was time for them to fall in love in the meantime," said MacLean.

That's right. He falls for the wrong sister. And she is a bit bewildered by her new situation:

"Her eyes had the look of girlish fascination at the unfamiliar world around her. She was such a child. Yet she had left her home and crossed an ocean with the expectation of becoming his wife. His wife? Dianna's baby sister. She had thought she'd meet his sons as their future stepmother. Good Lord. Did she know that Jacob, his stepson, was only four years younger than she?"

Some recognizable references are woven into the plot. Halifax gets a mention. But Cumberland Creek is fictional, I think. Madeleine, the "wrong sister," steps off the schooner and drinks in the landscape: "She squinted toward the rolling windswept expanse of grass that stretched for acres and acres into the distance, flanked on either side by ridges of wooded upland. This land, this magnificent land; it would be her home.

It hardly seemed possible."

The writer also borrows a nasty piece of real Nova Scotian weather and writes it into the story.

"I took a storm from the 1800s," said MacLean, "and made it happen in the 1700s." She chose the Saxby gale, a devastating storm from our provincial past. "When the dykes fail, it's based on that," she said.

MACLEAN: SELLING SENSUAL STORIES BY OUR SEA? SURE!

So her book includes immigration, ocean voyages, farming, wild weather, and windswept landscapes. Sounds like a Nova Scotian novel to me. Except it doesn't snow.

Being born a Doucette, MacLean also hopes to someday write of her Acadian heritage in Harlequin format. Imagine this plot conflict: a British soldier ordered to partake in the 1755 expulsion of the Acadians but he falls in love with an Acadian woman. Trauma and tears will no doubt follow and yet passion, as usual, will win out.

But first, *Adam's Promise* will bring Nova Scotian history to romance readers around the world. Should be good for tourism if not for literature. And if you're wondering which sister the Yorkshire farmer finally chooses to be his bride in Nova Scotia…well, don't ask me. The author wouldn't say. Maybe I'll get one of my sisters to read the story and tell me how it ends.

GOODBYE HITLER, HELLO DON MESSER

A Nova Scotian TV pioneer goes from Nazi Germany to celtic fiddling

---

From Hitler to Halifax, via Joey Smallwood's Newfoundland and the CBC's *Don Messer's Jubilee* program, Rolf Blei's career sure took some strange turns. A long time Haligonian, now deceased, Mr. Blei was eighty-seven when we spoke in 2001. His life had followed a zigzag path blazed by his skills as a technician in the infant days of television, film, and sound recording. It all began at the 1936 Berlin Olympics, one of the first public tests of the new invention, television.

There's black-and-white documentary footage of Adolf Hitler, standing stiff-backed in uniform, behind a row of early-model microphones, addressing the masses of thousands in the Olympic stadium. A parade of uniformed Nazi flag-wavers marches by on the runners' track below Hitler's viewing stand. The crowd cheers. Swastikas are everywhere. Right arms are jutted out, saluting. It was a strange time. And a young Rolf Blei was caught in the middle of it.

Sitting with his wife in his small, comfortable, suburban Halifax home, Blei spoke to me of that amazing day in that German stadium, over sixty years ago. He was a TV technician in training.

"I was allowed to carry these battery boxes and that's all I was allowed or assigned to do," said Blei. "I was a young student; twenty-two or twenty-three years old."

The Berlin Olympics was Hitler's platform for political propaganda, heard over radio and a crude television system that was to let government workers and others watch his speech. As a technical safety measure, the careful technicians arranged back-up microphones for Hitler's historic address.

BLEI: PART OF TV'S EARLIEST BEGINNINGS.

"There were always four microphones," Blei recalled.

The technical set-up was advanced for its day. Forty-five film cameras covered the athletic action, setting a standard for future TV coverage. "All these films, which were in film cameras around the track, were then processed in the truck," said Blei, his German accent still evident. The films were "scanned in the truck and then delivered to the sets in the government buildings in the city of Berlin."

The controversial German documentary maker, Leni Riefenstahl, was also there taking black-and-white footage for a propaganda film.

When war broke out, Blei became a lieutenant in Germany's air force. Part of his military duty was installing tape recorders—another new invention—in German aircraft to record recognizance information in the air. But eventually it all came to an end.

"I had to capitulate and went into a prisoner-of-war camp in Hamburg," he said.

When his British interrogators learned of his technical ability, they asked him: "Would you like to go and serve in the British forces network?"

Blei's response: "As a soldier?"

"'No, no, not as a soldier; as a manager of the station of the British army,'" said Blei, remembering his interrogators' words.

"'You speak very good English and you know the tape recorders,'" he recalled them saying.

So, he taught British broadcasters how to use tape recorders. Later, after the war, he was recruited from Germany by an unlikely business promoter.

"There was a trade commission coming over from Newfoundland under Joey Smallwood," said Blei. "We were seconded and went to St. John's to build a film studio."

He even did a personal favour for Newfoundland's pioneer premier.

"Joey wanted to have a radio in his house and he wanted a nice record player and so on. We made him a nice cabinet," he said.

Do not adjust your set. There's more to come. Rolf Blei moved to Nova Scotia when CBC Television in Halifax signed on the air on December 20, 1954.

"The start of broadcast television in Berlin was more political activated as anything else," he said, "not as loosely controlled as we have it here."

Then came the German technician's first brush with the unfamiliar Maritime sounds of Don Messer's music in the early days of the CBC's *Don Messer's Jubilee* program. Blei chuckled as he remembered. "It was some kind of a fiddle with a screeching, out of pitch altogether! I thought, 'Oh, what horrible music!'"

"That's how I learned about Messer's show," he said, "but today I love it!"

Many Maritimers will remember with fondness the popular Buchta Dancers on the Messer program of the 1950s and 1960s. "I met Gunther Buchta in the College Street studios," said Blei. Apparently the head of the dance troupe appealed to Blei, a fellow immigrant, to help him win his big break in Canadian TV.

"He said, 'I have a dance group, maybe we can have them on the Don Messer show,'" said Blei. And so, a Maritime Messer tradition was born.

In 1978, Blei retired from CBC TV, helped set up a radio station in the far north and voluntarily taught the technology in South America.

Whew! Now there's a television career worth recording.

ICELAND IN NEW SCOTLAND: A PEOPLE'S SURVIVAL

Ruins and reminiscences
reveal Icelanders' Nova Scotian experience

F rom a treeless land of volcanoes and ice they came to live in Nova Scotia's woods. From Iceland to New Scotland! It was a geographical and cultural shock for thirty Icelandic families—about two hundred people—who settled near Caribou Mines, Halifax County, in 1875. They called their settlement Markland, a familiar name from their Viking heritage. But their life here was anything but familiar.

The Icelandic Society of Nova Scotia released a new CD in 2002, *The Story of Markland*, which tells these brave settlers' saga in stirring narration and song. Musician Bill Stevenson's resonating voice describes the bitter conditions in 1873 that drove these rugged Icelanders from their homeland and eventually to Nova Scotia: "That year saw an unusually harsh winter with unmerciful blizzards, a very late and cold spring with never-ending arctic pack ice."

The recorded voice explains that "the pasture lands could not yield the life-sustaining grasses for the animals, and the fishing was very poor." It's a powerful tale well told. They were forced to leave Iceland and were lured to Nova Scotia.

The provincial government enticed the Icelanders to live in our forest with promises of a hundred acres of land each, a free log cabin, provisions, and tools. They were to grow crops to feed the gold miners at the then-prosperous Caribou Mines.

Dolly Belmore, 87, a retired schoolteacher living in that area, grew fascinated by the Icelanders' story. A few years ago she flew to Iceland to research it and learned how very unprepared those pioneers were.

"In Iceland, there are no natural forests," she told me. "So when they arrived here they had no idea what to do with a tree!"

"They were given an axe and a hoe," she said, "but they had to get someone from outside the village to show them how to cut down a tree."

The first group lived in one building called Iceland House before their cabins were built. They built the main settlement road; a dollar a day for back-breaking labour.

"Conditions were terrible," said Belmore, "they had to cut down huge trees and lift up boulders; there was nothing there *but* boulders! They weren't used to the flies and the darkness; Iceland has the midnight sun there," she said.

The Icelanders were literate and education was important to them. A diary and a census of Markland have been uncovered. They hired a Scottish teacher, and set up a school with twenty-five students at first, all under ten years old. It doubled as their Lutheran Church. They had a general store and a community council that held meetings.

"This man, Gudbrandur Erlendsson, studied medicine in his homeland so he was able to be the doctor," said Belmore. "He was a homeopath and practiced that in the settlement." Government promises of fine farm land suitable even for grape growing were misleading. The land was rocky and poor. One innovative settler drained a lake to find fertile soil for planting. Yet they all lived in poverty.

But the diary writer shows how the Icelanders appreciated Nova Scotia's wonderful wilderness, especially the unfamiliar seasonal changes.

"He talks about the birds on the trees, the squirrels, and the beauty of the land as he was driving through on his ox team, going to church to have his newest baby baptized," said Belmore.

"I think that shows it was a community like any other."

It was Dolly Belmore's dream to bring to life this old Icelandic settlement's heritage. She writes about it for a Manitoba-based Icelandic newspaper. Her society's website draws response from around the world.

When the society unveiled a cairn to the Markland pioneers in the summer of 2000, descendants of those settlers came by the busload from the United States to see just the grown-over stone foundations left in the woods between Caribou Mines and Mooseland, Halifax County. The Markland descendants were greatly moved by the experience.

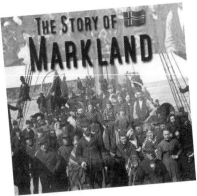

AN AUDIO MEMORIAL
TO NOVA SCOTIA'S ICELANDERS.

"It was wonderful," said Belmore, "they were just so excited. One old man, we almost had to carry away from the foundation, he was just so overcome with emotion," she said. "Most of them resort to tears when they see how their ancestors lived."

Alas, the Icelanders did not live for long on that rocky land. After seven years, they had all dispersed. But they prospered elsewhere: a nationally recognized Icelandic playwright and poet, and the first Icelandic-American senator (for North Dakota) had lived in Markland.

One Icelandic family resettled in Nova Scotia's Lockeport area. The original settler was a man named Erlendur Hoskuldsson. Hence, the Huskilsons; a well-known south shore name even today.

The *Story of Markland* CD and photos of the stone cairn and the descendants who came to see it are available at this website: *www.nova-scotia-icelanders.ednet.ns.ca.*

It is a fine, modern memorial to yet another courageous group of unique settlers who fought unfamiliar and harsh conditions to try building a new life in a new land that offered new hope: Nova Scotia.

AUNT JEMIMA OF NOVA SCOTIA

Our controversial link to the logo lady of the pancake box

This is a story of pride, prejudice, and pancakes. If you grew up eating Quaker Oats pancake products, you've seen Aunt Jemima: the smiling, bandanna-wearing, black lady of the logo. Some say she was from Nova Scotia. And she was, in a way.

Our Aunt Jemima was Dorothy—or Dot— Paris of New Glasgow. Hired by the Quaker Oats company to go on tour dressed as Aunt Jemima, Paris attended pancake promotion events at food stores and fairs in the 1950s. Her family keeps a photograph of her in full costume.

"She looks like she could have been the original Aunt Jemima," said her granddaughter, Vivian Thomas.

"She had on the attire: the bandanna on her hair, the crisp white dress and the apron over that."

Being Aunt Jemima was a unique job that took Dot Paris far afield from her small hometown of New Glasgow, where she had spent her whole life.

"She would tell us about her time and her travels from New Glasgow to Montreal, Ottawa and into the United States as well," said Thomas, "I think as far as Boston."

Thomas remembers her famous grandmother as a renowned cook;

much loved in the community, joyful, and personable. "Her personality was out of this world," said Thomas, "very kind. All my friends used to call her Nanny as well; doesn't matter what colour [they were]."

She was very much like the smiling, friendly "aunt" the commercial logo projects.

"She automatically made you feel part of the family," said Thomas.

But the logo was a corporate construction, inspired by a performer in an old minstrel show in the latter 1800s. There was no actual Aunt Jemima. Over the last century or so, black women were paid to appear in costume as Aunt Jemima. The first was Nancy Green, a former slave who appeared publicly at the World's Columbian Exposition in Chicago in 1893. She had an exclusive contract to cook pancakes, sing, and tell stories of the Old South.

Quaker Oats took over the company in 1926. Through the decades there have been several high-profile Aunt Jemimas appearing in radio and TV commercials, at Disneyland, and even on TV shows in New York.

Dot Paris was one of many Aunt Jemimas all over the continent. For her, it was just an interesting job she was good at, with lots of travel.

But some people attack the image she was portraying. Accused of supporting racial stereotypes, Quaker Oats modernized their old logo, lightening the skin, removing the bandanna, adding jewellery and slimming Jemima's face. The food company also founded a corporate award for black female entrepreneurs.

But in 1996, officials of a Texas town faced a backlash when they tried to promote the history of a local woman who once portrayed Aunt Jemima. Nova Scotian playwright David Woods spun a whole radio play from the inspiration of just seeing the photo of Dot Paris in her costume. *The Aunt Jemima Story* aired nationally on CBC Radio in the early 1990s.

Woods's play creatively takes the Aunt Jemima image to another level and explores the long history of racial issues behind black images used commercially.

Woods knew Dot Paris and respected her decision to play that role. He knew she had children to raise and worked two or three jobs in an era of limited opportunities for black women. However, he wanted to show that the pancake box logo—if you know the history behind it—was a very negative thing for some blacks.

"Initially these were not pleasant images for us," said Woods. "These were negative stereotypes imposed on our community," he said. "To be Aunt Jemima you had to be dark, large, big-chested and wear a bandanna."

AUNT JEMIMA OF NEW GLASGOW: PANCAKE POLITICS!

Woods thinks these commercially produced images, borrowed as they were from the era of slavery and racially offensive minstrel shows, were insulting. Nevertheless, white-owned companies used them to sell their products.

"So you can see," he said, "how that image was manufactured and maintained and in some ways is being presented as innocuous."

Vivian Thomas is a black woman and a working professional in Halifax who, today, sees both sides of the image issues inherent in her grandmother's role-playing job.

"I look back and say 'well done' and I'm very proud and honoured," said Thomas, "even though I look at it, at one point, as sort of stereotyping and a little derogatory and I'm sort of offended."

"But," she said, "back in that era, it took her to places she probably would never have seen."

Good point. Sometimes black-and-white issues aren't simply black and white.

As Aunt Jemima's granddaughter, Thomas is happy knowing that Dot Paris enjoyed her persona in the pancaking profession. "I'm glad she had the experience and that it was a positive one."

AMELIA EARHART
AND THE APOSTROPHE
CATASTROPHE

Major mapping mistakes in Nova Scotia

When in doubt, check the map, right? Normally that's good advice to an unsure traveller. But not when it comes to the official provincial maps of Nova Scotia. They contain mapping mysteries and miscues! Here are two examples for your cartographic consideration. One involves the famous female flyer, Amelia Earhart; the other, a punctilious punctuation problem.

First, the illegal apostrophe! Nova Scotia's road map for tourists is in violation of a long-held federal mapmaker's restriction banning the lowly apostrophe from Canada's maps, especially coastal maps like ours.

The anti-apostrophe convention goes back over a hundred years. It was strongly recommended by the Geographic Board of Canada in 1898.

In the early 1960s it became official policy under the Canadian Permanent Committee on Geographical Place Names. For real! Writer and researcher Parker Donham was not kidding when he tipped me to this mapping quirk.

David Wills, a Nova Scotian member of the national committee, told me the reasons varied for banning apostrophes on maps and charts. Confused cartographers had trouble sorting plural from possessive place names. Old-time printers with awkward presses struggled with the tiny apostrophe symbol.

Most importantly, the small but mighty apostrophe could be considered a navigational hazard! "In a coastal region such as Nova Scotia," said Wills, "the fact that an apostrophe could be thought of as an islet [a small island] or a lake would be an issue for mapmakers."

For sailors too!

As one-time Coordinator of Geographical Place Names with the department called Service Nova Scotia and Municipal Relations, Wills knows this punctuation peculiarity well. Even the exceptions.

"The only communities that officially have [possessive] apostrophes inserted in their names are Clark's Harbour, St. Peter's and the municipality of St. Mary's," said Wills.

"They were incorporated before the decision to rescind the apostrophes from place names in Nova Scotia." (Conjunctive apostrophes are used in French place names, such as Bras d'Or.)

So who defends the rights of this puny pawn of punctuation? The NDP, of course. The late, great socialist parliamentarian, Stanley Knowles, was vociferous in his opposition to the missing apostrophe on our map. The veteran underdog-defender had family roots going back four generations in this province, to Upper Woods Harbour, Shelburne County. When Knowles died in 1997, I spoke with Helen Gorham of the Samuel Woods Historical Society in Woods Harbour about the big political fuss Knowles once made about Nova Scotia's maps missing their apostrophes.

"He disputed the fact that the apostrophe had been left off the name of Woods Harbour," she said.

"He brought it up in the House of Commons and it was reported in the *Ottawa Journal*, March 7th, 1957."

Alas, failure. "I think we lost the cause," said Helen. Yes, Upper Woods Harbour is still apostrophe-less on Nova Scotia's official *Doers and Dreamers* maps.

But as the anti-apostrophe rule goes, the Nova Scotia tourist map I checked is, ah, all over the map. Some possessive places have it, some do not. Peggy's Cove has an apostrophe on the recent map I checked. But Gilberts Cove, near Digby, is apostrophe-free.

Some saintly sites seem to be blessed: St. Mary's Bay, between Yarmouth and Digby and St. Ann's Bay, Victoria County are both with apostrophe. And it is good. But St. Georges Bay, Antigonish County, is without an apostolic apostrophe, even though St. George's Channel near Dundee, Cape Breton, was not passed over. There's no uniformity at all. It's an apostrophe catastrophe!

But Marsha Andrews, spokesperson for our Department of Tourism and Culture, told me the tourist map is not an official Nova Scotia map, so rigid national rules need not apply. But she agreed that apostrophe uniformity might be a good thing. Whether on official archival maps of the province or on simple road maps for tourists. Maybe next year.

Now, map miscue number two regards Amelia Earhart, the famous first female to fly across the Atlantic, in 1926. She was a passenger on this trip, flying from Boston in a pontoon plane. Earhart's memoir *20 Hours, 40 Minutes* tells of the trio's landing in Halifax harbour, overnighting at a Dartmouth hotel, then taking off again.

First spotting Nova Scotia from the air, Earhart mentions a mysterious island near Pubnico Harbour, Shelburne County.

She writes: "Hooray! Nova Scotia at 8:55. Fear Island. We are flying at 2000. I can look down and see many white gulls flying over the green land. A few houses are clustered together and a dory is pulled up on the shore."

But there is no Fear Island. Earhart erred. There is a Lears Island— with an *S* (and no apostrophe)—in that location. David Wills found that the *S* was added in 1974. In Earhart's era, some maps featured it as just Lear. Likely, her map had it misspelled as Fear Island.

Or maybe she mistranscribed her own notes, which she had scribbled in the dark between two fuel tanks on a moving plane.

Oh, you may legitimately change a placename in Nova Scotia if you want. You may even lobby for an official apostrophe as the late Stanley Knowles did. But there are formal channels to go through.

Now if we could just properly punctuate our provincial highway signs! Tourists looking for Peggy's Cove are directed by our official signage to Peggys Cove instead. Maybe it's a government cost-saving measure but, really, how much extra paint could it take to add the apostrophe?

MARCONI'S MIRACLE ON OUR SHORES

Forget Newfoundland—radio messages started in Nova Scotia

This story is brought to you by the letter *S* and the number 100. In December 2001, the world celebrated the 100th anniversary of the first transatlantic wireless signal—a simple Morse Code *S*, three dots—being sent through the air, over the ocean and received on a copper kite wire at St. John's, Newfoundland. Guglielmo Marconi had done it! Global communication was beginning. But wait a minute. Stop the presses! (Or cease the transmission!) That was just a test on a temporary receiver. It was just one letter; a test signal. Two-way, global communication with actual coded words began here in Nova Scotia! Marconi achieved this world-changing event at Glace Bay, Cape Breton.

To be fair, Marconi's very first Morse code radio signal was sent and received over land in 1895 in his homeland, Italy. But his history-altering transatlantic achievement, linking old world with new, was a Nova Scotian first. No sooner had he heard that *S* signal arrive on Signal Hill in St. John's, he was kicked out of Newfoundland by the Anglo-American Telegraph Company, owners of the transatlantic underwater cable service. Who needs competition from a guy who can hear things from the air when you've paid to run a cable across the width of the Atlantic ocean? So, Mr. Marconi needed a new spot to set up his permanent message-sending station. He chose Nova Scotia.

There's a former physics teacher in Wolfville who has made Marconi his favourite research hobby. Henry Bradford retired from teaching physics at the Coast Guard school in Cape Breton. He was drawn to the world of physics by his youthful excitement over the magic of invisible radio waves travelling in the air.

From him I learned that the so-called father of radio was welcomed to Cape Breton by the father of the telephone, Alexander Graham Bell.

"Bell gave Marconi a standing invitation if he wanted to come to his Baddeck estate," said Bradford, "to do his experimental work if he so wished."

The radio pioneer came to Cape Breton but set up his shop at the point of land called Table Head at Glace Bay.

"He would have probably stayed in Newfoundland and built a permanent station, because his objective was a commercial wireless service, but the Anglo-American Telegraph Company in Newfoundland was quite upset," he said.

"They could see this [wireless] would be a competitor," said Bradford, "so their lawyers told Marconi he would have to cease his experiments."

Marconi crossed the Cabot Strait from Newfoundland on Christmas Eve 1901, arriving Christmas Day to a welcoming party on the dock at North Sydney.

The Canadian and Nova Scotian governments knew a good thing when they saw it.

"They gave him the Table Head land for free and they also gave him about $80,000, which was sufficient to build the station," said Bradford.

At Table Head, Marconi sent the world's "first transatlantic telegraph messages as opposed to a test signal—these were complete messages—transmitted from Glace Bay to the corresponding station at Cornwall England," said Bradford. "A huge accomplishment!"

The hundredth anniversary of that historic message was in December 2002. Actually, Marconi himself didn't send the first official over-the-ocean wireless telegraph message. He allowed a journalist that honour. A London *Times* writer tapped out the short coded greeting to his editors in England. With the new medium, good media relations had already begun. As Marshall McLuhan might have said, in that case, "the media sent the message."

But Marconi's goal was to set up a permanent message-sending business. Which he did. It was actually a little south of his Glace Bay site, at a site now called Marconi Towers, in Cape Breton. His new station there was even bigger and more powerful. Its huge towers of zigzagging wooden supports held up an array of wires, an aerial connected to the station below. It opened in 1907, charging the public to send messages overseas.

It lasted until 1945, sending telegraph messages from the interior of the continent to Europe via Morse code dots and dashes. A receiving station was set up at Louisbourg so messages could arrive while others were being sent.

Soon, with other inventors of course, pioneer wireless radio became a voice medium. From that grew the old radio legacy that so many today are fond of recalling.

"I can remember back in the 1930s when we listened to the radio—CHNS in Halifax—there was a program that came on in the evenings sponsored by the Marconi Company," said Bradford, reflecting.

MARCONI, LOOKING VERY DASHING. AND DOTTING.

"Their slogan was 'Marconi: the greatest name in radio!' so I had heard of Marconi from that time," he said.

Just think, this great inventor's pioneer wireless work, here on our very shores, initiated the science of shortwave, television, satellites, cell phones, wireless email and two-way transmissions into space!

WHO WROTE "THE BALLAD OF SPRINGHILL"?

How a famous folkie finally met the miner in her song

In the town of Springhill, Nova Scotia
Down in the dark of the Cumberland mine
There's blood on the coal and the miners lie
In roads that never saw sun nor sky

"The Ballad of Springhill" is a well-known, oft-sung, and cherished piece of folk music that tells the true story of the Springhill Miracle. But the story of the song itself is worth a telling too. From the famous 1960s American trio Peter, Paul and Mary to Cape Breton's beloved Men of the Deeps miners' choir, many have sung and recorded the mournful tune—here and abroad—over the past four decades or so. But you might be surprised to learn who wrote it, and how.

The songwriter was motivated by the international news of the Springhill coal mine's collapse. As the song goes on to say, it was "late in the year of '58." A disastrous bump, or shift of earth, deep below ground left dozens of coal miners lying dead in the deeps. A few lucky men were trapped alive in cramped spaces in the black belly of the mine. A vigil of weeping wives and worried townsfolk formed above ground. CBC Television carried the dramatic mine-rescue story around the world; a TV first. After six and half days trapped below, twelve men were brought up alive, on live TV. Two days later, seven more rescued miners appeared. Tragedy and miracle were mixed.

The famous folk singer, Peggy Seeger, sister of that other famous folkie, Pete Seeger, and partner of the late singer-songwriter Ewan Mac-Coll, was in her early twenties in 1958. Her musical muse was moved by the news out of Springhill that year.

She followed the mine-rescue drama while living in France, having been thrown out of England for playing the banjo without a work visa. But that was before she and MacColl made music history together.

Songwriter Allister MacGillivray's book, *The Nova Scotia Song Collection*, describes how Seeger and MacColl developed a revolutionary form of song called the radio ballad. Seeger, also known for her song, "Gonna Be an Engineer," recorded more than three dozen albums over her career. "The Ballad of Springhill" has long been one of her most requested tunes. At age sixty-nine, she sings it still. And when I reached her by phone at her home in North Carolina, she still remembered how she was inspired to write the song even though, in 1958, she was an ocean away from the little mining town of Springhill, Nova Scotia.

"One night I was watching the French television and on comes this program about Springhill showing how the women and the children were at the minehead, and there's weeping and breast-beating," said Seeger.

"The miners had apparently been down there for a day or two and the television crew had arrived," she said, "and this apparently was the first time a mine disaster had been televised worldwide."

Joan Watson was reporting for CBC at the time. "A terrific bump was felt," she reported, "signalling once again that disaster had struck."

"One hundred and forty-five men are over 13,000 feet down; deep under the town tonight," she told the world.

Seeger was transfixed by the human drama unfolding on her TV screen. Ewan MacColl had crossed the English Channel to visit her at her place of exile in France.

"I had never been down a mine, and he had, so he added one of the verses," she said.

Ewan came up with verse four:

> *Down at the coal face, miners working*
> *The rattle of the belt and the cutter's blade,*
> *Rumble of rock and the walls close round.*
> *Living and the dead men two miles down.*

"That gave it its mine atmosphere," said Seeger.

But Seeger wrote the following lyrics about one of the rescued miners she saw on TV:

> *Three days passed and the lamps gave out*
> *And Caleb Rushton, he up and said:*
> *"There's no more water nor light nor bread,*
> *So we'll live on songs and hope instead."*

This song story has a modern-day twist: In the late 1990s, while driving into Nova Scotia to perform in Canso, Peggy Seeger, who had never been to Springhill, was surprised to see the highway sign for the town.

"I thought, 'Whoa! I'm right near this place,'" she said.

She nearly caused a traffic accident. "I swerved over to the right and went into Springhill and I found Caleb Rush-

ton! And this is forty years after the fact!"

The famous folksinger and the retired coal miner and his wife had coffee together.

"We had a wonderful meeting; I was just so thrilled," said Seeger. "We talked about the disaster and his wife talked about what it was like to be there waiting for him to come back."

In her song, Seeger also wrote:

> *Eight days passed and some were rescued,*
> *Leaving the dead to lie alone*
> *Through their lives they dug a grave*
> *Two miles of earth for a marking stone.*

Nova Scotians know and love the song and sing it at kitchen parties and community concerts. It's a Nova Scotian classic. But I'm sure few of us knew how it came about or who wrote its stirring lyrics. Who would have guessed the songwriter was an American living in France who probably couldn't find Springhill on a map at the time? But that suits the songwriter just fine.

"I love it," said Seeger over the long distance line. "That just is so heart-warming. Wordsworth said he'd give anything to have written an anonymous song. It means that you have written it the way people think, and people sing it naturally. I like it."

To readers in Springhill, Peggy Seeger asked me to pass on her best wishes, because her song is your story.

HOW MOBY-DICK GOT SO BIG

The Nova Scotian who made Melville's novel a literary classic

W hat a fascinating chain of connections I stumbled into by accident: From a famous coffee franchise to one of the great literary classics of the last century, with a stopover at Dartmouth's early Quaker history, and a final fall into the remarkable life of a Nova Scotian man of letters.

It's odd, the abundance of zigzaggy stories like this that are found on this seabound coast of ours. It's as if this place secretly harbours a magical crossroads of coincidence that twists our timeline into a double helix. Here, history doesn't simply repeat itself, it overlaps on itself!

This story search started out innocently enough; a simple email from Dr. Andrew Starzomski who works in Dartmouth. He's an expert in forensic psychology but he turned to me to help solve this puzzle. Recently returned to Nova Scotia, he picked up a book on Dartmouth history and learned that the community that grew up across the harbour from Halifax included an early settler named Starbuck. The good doctor wrote, "I think there is a link between that person and the story behind the name of the Starbucks Coffee Company based in Seattle."

Looking into an alleged link between Dartmouth's past and the famous high-end java empire, Starbucks, turned out to be a "tall" order of "grande" proportions. Much more grande than I expected.

Let's start with that Starbuck name. The Starbuck family in Dartmouth's past was one of twenty-four families of Quakers who settled in the harbourfront town in the late 1780s. They were whalers who moved here from the American island of Nantucket, Massachusetts. That's why you often hear on CBC Radio's morning traffic reports that "the traffic at the Macdonald bridge tolls is back to Nantucket." It's not that the traffic line stretches to Massachusetts. It's a street name honouring Dartmouth's early immigrant whaler families from that island.

Those early Dartmouth whalers were a rugged bunch. Just ask Dartmouth history researcher and author, Doug Trider.

"They tore down their houses in Nantucket, put them on whale ships, took them up to Dartmouth and rebuilt them," said Trider.

"There were several Starbucks," he said, "it was a rather big family."

"They were very influential because they were very wealthy and one of them in particular was the owner of several whaling ships, Samuel Starbuck."

MELVILLE: NOVA SCOTIA BROUGHT HIS WHALE TO THE SURFACE.

Well, that would be interesting if the famously overpriced, image-conscious coffee franchise located within the stores of Canada's giant bookseller chain was somehow named for a Dartmouth whaler guy! So I looked further to learn more.

I turned to Karen Koonings, the public relations spokesperson for Starbucks Coffee in Toronto. I figured she could answer that question faster than you can say "swiss mocha decaf espresso with chocolate sprinkles."

"The first store was called Starbucks Coffee, Tea and Spices," said Koonings when I reached her by phone at the Starbucks head office. "The original owners of the company named it after Herman Melville's *Moby-Dick*," she said. "There's a character, the coffee-loving first mate, in that book who is actually called Starbuck. So that is why they chose the name."

My first thought was, "That's really cool!"
If the yuppie coffee shops were named for a
character in the famous whale novel, and
the Starbuck in question was a whaler in
the early town of Dartmouth, then the
Moby-Dick character was named for a
Nova Scotian. This was huge!

The next step was to figure out
why Herman Melville, the author of
the classic, Moby-Dick, would name
one of his main characters after a guy
from Nova Scotia. The Dartmouth history enthusiast has his theory. It involved
one of the Dartmouth Quakers; a whaler
named Seth Coleman who was a friend of
the Dartmouth Starbuck family.

**DALHOUSIE'S MACMECHAN
MADE MOBY-DICK REALLY BIG.**

"Melville was hired on to work on this
whaling ship that Coleman had," said
Trider, "and he became a boat steersman, they call it."

Whoa! This was huger. Herman Melville gained some of the whaling experience that inspired his now-famous novel by sailing under a
Nova Scotian captain. Awesome. He learned the ropes of whaling and
then wrote about what he knew. This could be our link to an American literary masterpiece. Plus, Melville may have met Coleman's friend
Starbuck and so chose that name for his upstanding firstmate character
who serves the troubled Captain Ahab in the novel.

But Melville experts say that is unlikely. I tracked down two Melvillians by calling the editor of *Leviathan*, the academic journal of the
International Melville Society at Hofstra University in New York. You
won't believe this one: He told me the highly regarded husband and
wife team of Melville experts I should talk to about this alleged Dartmouth connection happen to live in…Dartmouth! Another twist in
this whale tale.

These internationally recognized Melvillians are both retired from
Halifax universities. Dr. Fred Kennedy was a librarian at Dalhousie and

Dr. Joyce Kennedy taught English at Mount Saint Vincent. Both are literary historians. They don't live very far from Nantucket Avenue or from Dartmouth's Starbucks coffee shop, for that matter. It's a small world when it comes to the big whale.

I met these two *Moby-Dick* enthusiasts at their Dartmouth home. The brass whale-shaped door knocker helped me find the right house. Inside, they showed me their *Moby-Dick* books, posters, trinkets, cartoons, statuettes, and souvenirs. The spirit of Melville permeates their living quarters. We had a fine chat over coffee. (Homebrewed, not takeout.)

Joyce Kennedy was quick to shoot down the Dartmouth–Starbuck connection theory. Sure the Dartmouth Starbuck came originally from Nantucket, which is where Melville's whaling ship sails from in the novel, but that's not saying much. Apparently Nantucket at the time had as many whalers named Starbuck as Cape Breton had coal miners named MacDonald. With his high seas whaling background, the author might have heard the common Nantucket family name anywhere in his travels. As well, the Coleman who hired on Melville as a boatsteerer was not the same one who knew the Dartmouth whaler named Starbuck. It was a distant relative of his, Captain John B. Coleman, who was master of the vessel *Charles and Henry* out of Nantucket. In 1842, decades after the Starbuck clan landed at Dartmouth, this Coleman picked up Melville off a beach in the South Seas. Captain John Coleman was Dartmouth born, however, so Nova Scotia at least holds that little claim to Melvillian fame. I learned that much from *Whales and Destiny*, by Edouard A. Stackpole, a book from Dr. Kennedy's library.

The Kennedys' academic diligence really sank my boat on this fun Starbuck connection. But, just as quickly, they refloated my interest with even greater buoyancy. Joyce Kennedy surprised me with this amazing twist to *Moby-Dick* history:

"The only reason anybody would ask this question about Starbucks today," she said "is that you've got Starbucks coffee house because of *Moby-Dick*, and you've got *Moby-Dick* being known, when it had been buried basically in North America, because of the Nova Scotian Mac-Mechan."

Hold on now. Hard to port. Who was this MacMechan fellow? It turns out that he is a figure in our past who provides us with a Nova Scotia–*Moby-Dick* relationship that blows the alleged coffee connection out of the water. Archibald MacMechan was a Dalhousie University professor at the turn of the century who, according to the two Kennedys, was responsible for making *Moby-Dick* the classic novel it is hailed as today. He made Moby-Dick a household name.

MacMechan discovered Melville's nearly forgotten whaling novel and loved it. His passion for salty stories of the sea was strong. For many years he enjoyed collecting the sea stories of this province. It seems MacMechan was something of a Nova Scotia know-it-all, you might say. Fred Kennedy drew the comparison.

"He did what you do," he said to me, "in the sense that you go around hunting down stories. In MacMechan's case he was interested in sea stories. He'd go to customs houses and libraries and archives in places like Liverpool and Shelburne and he'd find out where old sailing masters who were retired were living and he'd investigate their stories; true stories of the sea connected with Nova Scotia."

Herman Melville was known for his other sea stories, but the quintessential sea saga titled *Moby-Dick; or The Whale*, was his lesser-known novel. Few in North America had heard of it, let alone read it. A handful of academics in Britain knew of it, but the 1851 novel was pretty much off the literary chart; virtually unknown; lost in the sea of unread, undiscovered, unappreciated literary works.

But as early as 1890, the Halifax professor, who chose to teach at Dalhousie partly because he loved the proximity to the sea, began promoting Melville's dramatic whaling tale. Captain Ahab's psychotic, vengeful pursuit of the mysterious great white whale was a story that was, to MacMechan's mind, brilliantly conceived and artfully told. MacMechan wrote to Melville, hoping to have his assistance in reviving the novel. Melville's written response to MacMechan is stored in a file in a vault at the Dalhousie University archives. Melville letters are not common and are worth thousands. Essentially, this Melville letter offers a cordial reply to MacMechan, thanking him for his interest. But Melville backs out of any future involvement, citing old age and ill health.

Undaunted by that letter, Archibald MacMechan launched a one-man *Moby-Dick* promotion campaign that lasted about thirty years. In 1899 he published an academic journal article called "The Best Sea Story Ever Written." In it, he trumpeted Melville's novel as an artfully written piece of work with unique merits that never received its due recognition. MacMechan loved the book. In his letter to Melville, stored at Harvard, he had written that he had "read and reread *Moby-Dick* with increasing pleasure on every perusal." MacMechan poured out his great enthusiasm for the book in the pages of his academic article. In 1914, he published that article again in a commercially-available book called *The Life of a Little College and Other Papers*. That volume was purchased and read by the general public.

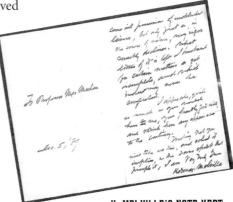

H. MELVILLE'S NOTE KEPT AT DALHOUSIE UNIVERSITY

As well, MacMechan urged the reading of *Moby-Dick* through his social and academic circles. He had contacts at Harvard and other universities. He mailed out copies of his published praise for *Moby-Dick*, winning over new Melville fans in distant places.

"He presented copies of that to people at the National Library of Scotland, and Ireland, and scholars and students," said Joyce Kennedy.

"He had people thanking him and saying they must read this thing, and others saying they never heard of it but, 'boy it really sounds like it's good,' and they'll have to read it."

The word spread far and wide. Academics in high places responded positively. Then, writers began writing about MacMechan's writing on Melville's writing.

"The review of this thing was in newspapers all over North America because of MacMechan," said Dr. Kennedy.

This college professor in out-of-the-way Nova Scotia waged his campaign to recognize *Moby-Dick* up into the 1920s. Then, he was heartened to see his lifelong effort had finally paid off. Herman Melville's *Moby-Dick* was by then a text read by students in public schools.

Years later, after MacMechan's death, the novel would become required reading at universities. Its themes would later launch Melville associations, learned journals, and great intellectual debates. The Ahab and whale characters would become icons in twentieth-century culture. And of course, the inevitable: *Moby-Dick* motion pictures, *Moby-Dick* comic books and colouring books; *Moby-Dick* pins and placemats, trinkets and treasures. The hunt for the great white whale is an image even those who haven't read the novel are aware of. It's ingrained in society now. But in the 1850s, when the story was first written, it foundered and disappeared from view almost as soon as it was released.

"In North America, it sort of sank," said Joyce Kennedy. "*Moby-Dick* didn't get great reviews in the beginning and then it seemed to disappear from existence for a number of years. Now it is a household word!"

"And I think," she said, "that the one to kick off the twentieth-century revival really was MacMechan. Nobody in the United States did the job that MacMechan did."

This Nova Scotian college professor had the determination of Captain Ahab, but with better luck. Like a committed whaler, Archibald MacMechan pursued this big fish story for a long time, put up a good fight, and finally landed it for all to see and enjoy. And to think it was almost the one that got away!

NOVA SCOTIA'S NEVERFAILS

A rock-solid remembrance of the men who took Passchendaele

A 6,800-kilogram (15,000-pound) piece of Nova Scotia was rolled onto a Belgian farmer's cornfield in late October 2001. The monolith of granite was erected to stand in the centre of a circle of death. Back when the pretty patchwork fields all around that scenic spot were bogs of mud and blood, 148 Nova Scotia Highlander soldiers died there in the Battle of Passchendaele in October 1917. The new monument of Nova Scotian stone, carved by Heritage Memorials in Windsor and shipped overseas, was unveiled in that place to remember the heroics of the 85th Nova Scotia Highlanders Battalion, known as the Neverfails.

The nickname was fitting. Their reputation began at the brutal battle for Vimy Ridge, about six months earlier. Easter Monday morning, the Canadians pushed up that sloppy slope with a metal canopy of constant shellfire close over their heads as protection, and steady German fire raining down on them. Hill 145 was a crucial objective to take. The scene was a gory maelstrom. Men were falling all around.

At Vimy, the soldiers of the 85th were new; unblooded. They were just shovel swingers getting oriented to the front lines while digging trenches and tunnels. According to Steve Kempton, chairman of the

Nova Scotia Highlanders Heritage Society and grandson of a World War One Highlander, the commanding officers at Vimy were running out of men to send over the top.

"They looked around and said, 'Well, who do we have that we can throw into this?'" said Kempton. "The 85th was there," he said, "so they exchanged picks and shovels for rifle and bayonet."

The Neverfails were born.

"They took the Ridge, Hill 145," said Kempton. "In fact the ground the 85th captured is where the current monument at Vimy Ridge, those impressive towers, now stands." The Passchendaele battle that followed, known as the Third Battle of Ypres, began October 30 and continued through November 2, 1917. The Canadian corps attacked at 5:30 a.m. under a blood-red sky. Six hundred of the 85th Battalion fought. Two hundred and eighty were wounded. The one hundred and forty-eight killed died within a short radius of the monument site. The battlefield was left "completely denuded of any vegetation or buildings."

Kempton's reading of the battalion's history tells him that "no two bricks stood on each other in the town of Passchendaele." Rain turned mud into a dangerous soup. "They lost guns, horses and men that simply disappeared in the mud if they fell off the duck boards," he said.

But the Highlanders didn't fail. They achieved what the Allies had been trying for months. They broke through the strongly held German defences.

The impressive new Nova Scotian memorial replaces the crumbling monument erected there in 1919 by surviving comrades of the fallen. Bringing in that new stone marker was like a changing of the granite guards; a handing off of the silent watch kept over Nova Scotia's war dead. Though it is on private farm land, the monument's large base was preserved as official Belgian State land. That base was replaced by the 11th Engineering Battalion of the Belgian Army. They have not forgotten what our soldiers did to help liberate their country.

Steve Kempton's grandfather, Sgt. Stanley S. Kempton of Harmony, Queens County, was a member of the Neverfails and lost many friends on that field. But he wasn't part of that fight. He was taken out of action in the previous battle by a German with a fast trigger finger. "He saw the German soldier bring his weapon up and he tried to bring his up and he saw the German get his shot off before he did," said Kempton.

"The bullet struck him in his right chest and went through his wallet, which probably saved his life. It perforated his wallet," he said, "through pictures from home, that kind of thing. It laid him open four inches long, two inches wide, an inch deep."

Miraculously, Sgt. Kempton survived. He recovered in an army hospital.

"My dad still has the wallet and the photos," said Kempton, "you can see the holes."

"There's one right through the picture of his sister! So he sent those with a letter home and said, 'I'm only giving you these photos on the condition that you send me some more back over,'" said Kempton, with a chuckle.

The old monument plaque bearing the less fortunate Highlanders' names is now stored at the Citadel in Halifax. The shiny new plaque on the smooth granite memorial in Belgium was unveiled to a contingent of about seventy-five Canadians, including our Minister of Veterans' Affairs and some Nova Scotia Highlanders

A PIECE OF NOVA SCOTIA IN A BELGIAN FIELD.

from the First and Second Battalion. Belgian dignitaries attended with a young Belgian school group. They came to remember those who fell. And Steve and his father were also present, for the same reason.

The logistics to fund, erect, and rededicate the private, non-government war memorial took the Highlanders Society some years. It cost a bundle to get that big rock over there. But, like their ancestors and heroes, the Neverfails, the society achieved its objective despite adversity. Before the Belgian rededication ceremony, Steve Kempton was looking forward to shifting his thoughts beyond the logistics of the physical stone marker itself.

"I think once it is over and done," said Kempton, "I will take a moment on my own and quietly contemplate what happened October 30, 1917."

Lest we forget.

A TINY TELEPHONE
IN THE DEEPS

An inventor helps rescue trapped men in Moose River's mine

"Herman Magill is dead. Two others, Dr. D. E. Robertson and Albert Scadding of Toronto, Ontario, are still in the depths of the Moose River mine late this afternoon."

That sombre message, in the tired but deliberate voice of broadcaster J. Frank Willis, delivered news of a Nova Scotian coal mine collapse—live from the remote mine site at Moose River—to over seven hundred North American radio stations that broadcast his reports around the clock. The crisis began began April 12, 1936 and coverage of it helped to launch network radio in Canada: the CBC. But it was another, newly invented, communication device that made the difference for the men trapped 43 metres (141 feet) below where the underground water was rapidly rising.

The gold mine's owner, Magill, was entombed with Robertson, a mine shareholder and Scadding, a mine employee. They had been inspecting the mine on Easter Sunday when they heard unusually loud noises. They tried a rapid ascension but, part way up the elevator shaft, the earth shook. Rock and timber crashed down on them. The three men survived, trapped in a dark, wet space where they set a small, smoky fire to signal those above that they were alive.

Word went out. An army of Nova Scotian draegermen and newspaper reporters poured into the site in the woods of Halifax County. Premier Angus L. Macdonald was

"JEFF" JEFFERSON: THE INVENTOR OF A TELEPHONE IN A FLASHLIGHT.

on the scene. The RCMP and soon the wives of the men below arrived as teams of rescue miners worked at digging down to the trapped men. They knew it would take days.

Over the course of the crisis, Magill would develop pneumonia in the damp underground and die. A diamond drill bit would be used to bore a long, narrow hole down to the two remaining men. Soup and coffee would be poured down the pipe. But the two weakened and isolated men left alive in that dark space needed a way to communicate with the surface; to know that those above were working to save them, to hear their wives' comforting voices, and to update rescuers on the dangerous, shifting conditions below.

The morning of the mine collapse, the head of Maritime Telegraph and Telephone Company was called out of church in Halifax. He immediately contacted his engineer at MT&T, William Jefferson, known as "Jeff" Jefferson. He and his technician, Bill Boak, were told to come up with a tiny telephone that could fit down a three-quarter-inch pipe! They got started.

Jefferson's solution was ingenious. "Dad always carried a very small flashlight which looked a bit like a fat pen," said Stephen Jefferson, the engineer's son. "He simply took his flashlight, gutted it, and stuffed the gear into that thing," he said as we talked at his Halifax home.

To supply that "gear," the tiny parts required, some Halifax storeowners opened their closed shops that Sunday. After two failed attempts, the tiny telephone was ready; a tube, wrapped in black fabric tape, with a wire on one end.

"But one of their problems, because it was pouring rain out there at Moose River most of the time, was to keep the thing dry," said Jefferson, who grew up hearing his father tell this story. "When father was reporting back at the dining room table on his activities, he said they used a balloon [to keep the device waterproof] but, when we grew up, we found out that really they used a condom."

THE INVENTION: A TIGHT SQUEEZE DOWN A PIPE.

The tiny, tubular, telephone transmitter was dropped on a long wire down the narrow pipe. Actually it was just half a telephone; a transmitter, with no receiver to hear messages. *Yes* and *no* replies from the surface were a bang or two bangs on the pipe or a hefty shout into it.

But the weak men trapped in the deeps had only to speak their concerns and questions into Jefferson's small transmitter. Word came from below of the threatening water level. It was, according to Willis, "creeping slowly through a thousand fissures in the crushed and broken walls of the mine." The broadcaster told radio listeners, "that now sends us the greatest warning: the water is rising!"

The underground transmitter was a lifeline for the fearful men below. It helped reassure them that the rescuers were on their way and would be there soon.

"The wives would be telling their husbands that they loved them," said Jefferson, "and would be praying for them and hoping for them." He also read that "as days wore on...the wives got their husbands to dictate their wills to them" over the miniature microphone. Things looked bleak as the days crawled by. But then, the Moose River miracle!

Eleven days after the mine collapse, the draegermen broke through to Robertson and Scadding and brought them up to fresh air and a large cheering crowd. Cameras flashed, doctors rushed to their aid, and Frank Willis informed the world. It was over! The men were safe.

Stephen Jefferson, himself a retired telephone company employee, thinks his father's clever invention helped to keep those men alive. "They would not have been able to know that the rescue shaft was going well because they couldn't hear the men digging," he said. Without that communication device, "they wouldn't know how far away they were; they would simply give up and die."

"A lot of people have said," said Jefferson, "that had it not been for that telephone, they would not have brought two men out of that mine alive."

THE NEW YORK MAYOR WHO RULED CAPE BRETON

Why a Big Apple mayor took a bite out of Nova Scotia

After September 11, 2001, we heard so much of the powerful position of mayor of New York City that it is interesting to learn of the feisty New York mayor who once became a powerful leader in Nova Scotia. David Mathews was the last Loyalist mayor of the Big Apple, in the days of the American Revolution. Some say he even schemed to assassinate George Washington.

Mathews was New York's mayor as the Americans fought to take that remaining British bastion during their War of Independence in the 1770s. His story is well told by Cape Breton historian Dr. Bob Morgan in the *Dictionary of Canadian Biography*.

But I learned about Mayor Mathews from a history researcher who, like Mathews himself, is British born, lived in New York, and also became a Cape Bretoner: David Newton.

"Mathews had been arrested," said Newton, "because of his implication in the plot to kill Washington."

This mayor may have been the bagman in the assassination scheme. "He allegedly contributed £100 sterling, which was a lot of money in those days," said Newton.

The Loyalist mayor was thrown into his own city jail, near the former site of the World Trade Center towers. He was accused of financing the infamous Hickey Plot.

According to Newton, Hickey was one of George Washington's soldiers and bodyguards. There were two alleged attempts on Washington's life: one involved poisoning his peas; the other, a plan to kidnap the general while he visited his mistress. But the plot either fizzled or failed. Relocated to jail in Connecticut, Mayor Mathews proved what a quarrelsome irritant he could be. "He was highly unpopular in Connecticut with the authorities and made himself a thoroughly unwelcome prisoner," said Newton. "The whole town was relieved when he managed to escape."

The clever politician gained his freedom by bribing guards. He was back in his mayor's chair in New York by December 1776, after the famous American Declaration of Independence had been signed on July 4 of that year. But the British had reoccupied New York and had driven Washington's troops out.

Mathews ruled over this big-city British holdout while protective British war ships sat off the harbour mouth. A large portion of New York's population was loyal to the crown. But it was a time of paranoia and nervousness; they were an island of loyalty surrounded by the strong, newly born American nation. After a peace treaty was signed in 1783, New York was turned over to the new United States. Loyalists were allowed—or encouraged—to leave, and they sailed by the shipload up to Nova Scotia.

The ambitious Mathews applied to become attorney general of the province, in Halifax. Turned down for that job, he became attorney general of the colony of Cape Breton and a deadly opponent and irritant of the colonial governor, J. F. W. DesBarres.

It appears Mathews was just not a nice guy at all. According to Newton, one New York judge's opinion of this Cape Breton attorney general was that he was "a person low in estimation as a lawyer, profligate, abandoned, extravagant, dissipated, indigent, extravagant, luxurious, head over heels in debt, and with a large family as extravagant and voluptuous as himself."

It's not surprising then that Mathews clashed harshly with his boss,

Governor DesBarres. "He was effective in seeing DesBarres kicked out," said Newton. "He went back to England and Mathews became chief administrator of the island for a while."

This former mayor of New York became somewhat of an iron-fisted mayor of Cape Breton!

It was the 1780s and Mathews enjoyed the power, using the attorney general's office to benefit his friends and family. When a Rev. Cossit crossed him, Mathews had the man of the cloth jailed on debt charges. But the minister had the last laugh.

Not long after the skirmish with Rev. Cossit, Mathews died and, the story goes, the minister refused to allow the body to be interred in the church cemetery.

So where is this former New York mayor buried? That's where a modern-day twist in this tale comes to light. You see, David Newton and his wife Pam—also a Cape Breton history researcher—have some coincidental connections to the late Mayor Mathews's story.

"Our background is divided," Newton admitted of his spouse. "I'm from England and she's from New York City—of long-established patriot or rebel connections," said Newton with a chuckle.

On top of that familial link, he also discovered that the farm he bought in Cape Breton is also tied to this tale.

"Mathews is believed to be buried at Amelia Point, very close to our own place," he said.

What are the odds? A British-born researcher and a New Yorker research a British-born mayor of New York; only to find they live very near to where he lies. I've said it before. History sure does take some strange twists through time in this unique place. That's Nova Scotia for you.

THE TIDAL PULL OF HOME

Two centuries later, a Nova Scotian clan comes full circle

Ask any Bluenose-blooded cottage dweller which spot he'd prefer, our beautiful sea-bound coast or a crowded bedroom community of Toronto, and then stand back. You might get hurt by the blast of the response. Of course, there's no comparison. Not now. But perhaps at one time. I give you: the link between Nova Scotia and the mighty Oakville, Ontario, esteemed for some years as the community with the highest income per capita in Canada.

A thirty-minute train ride from the Big Smoke, Oakville spreads itself widely; a flat town of burgeoning industry, development and wealth. It's home to brick mansions, landscaped estates and shiny BMWs. Gleaming yachts are moored at the mouth of Sixteen Mile Creek at Lake Ontario. The CN Tower rises in the distance. This successful, excessful Upper Canadian suburban town sprang from the humble hard work of a Nova Scotian lad from Jordan Bay, Shelburne County: William Chisholm.

Colourful flower gardens on a hill near the creek surround the brick Georgian building that is Oakville's museum, known as Erchless, on the founder's former property. He bought the land in 1827.

William Chisholm was born a Bluenose boy in 1788. His father, a United Empire Loyalist, later moved the family from Shelburne County to a farm in Burlington, Ontario. Chisholm grew up to become a powerhouse of entrepreneurship. He saw the value of the Sixteen Mile

Creek site, formerly land of Mississauga Indians. He purchased it from the Crown, using its great oaks to build ships. A family story says that the aboriginals called William "Chief White Oak," hence Oakville's name. This I learned while visiting the town's museum.

"William set about to build the town of Oakville," said museum interpreter, Anne Bobyk.

"He was our first developer," she said, irony intended. "In one year," said Bobyk, "he had moved his shipyard from Burlington, dredged the mouth of the river, started to build the piers, had a few warehouses under construction and had launched his first ship out at the mouth of the harbour."

This Maritimer took "going down the road" seriously!

The interpreter and I were sitting in the old Chisholm home, where six generations of Chisholms had come and gone. They were all very industrious, taking after their patriarch, William of Nova Scotia. He started Oakville's first shipbuilding, lumber mill, grist mill, customs house and (one might say, "of course") tavern!

He was an elected MP in Upper Canadian politics. As a military man with the York Militia, Chisholm had taken part in the capture of Detroit in 1812. Politically, Chisholm supported, then revolted against, William Lyon Mackenzie. He commanded the left flank in the infamous advance on Mackenzie's rebels at Montgomery's Tavern in Toronto.

Despite his successes, poor William Chisholm died bankrupt after a hydropower deal failed in his final years. Nevertheless the Chisholm clan prospered in his memory.

CHISHOLM'S HOME: OAKVILLE'S FOUNDER FROM SHELBURNE CO.

His great-granddaughter, Hazel Chisholm, published a thick history of Oakville. While researching the book, something magical happened to her. Arriving in Shelburne County, the land of her Chisholm forefathers, she fell in love with her family's ancestral homeland and so spent summers on Shelburne Harbour, writing. With time, she moved there altogether.

Her daughter, Nancy Hart, the original William Chisholm's great-great-granddaughter, also took to Shelburne County, at first just to care for her mother, Hazel. But after Hazel

NANCY HART: HOME, AFTER FIVE GENERATIONS.

Chisholm passed away, Nancy chose to stay living by the sea. After five generations, Nova Scotia somehow still felt like home for this Chisholm family.

I asked Nancy why her mother, the writer, wished to be on this coastline in such a rural spot after a long life lived in lavish Oakville.

"She really felt very deeply her roots here and she came back here and spent the last two years of her life here," she said.

Nancy herself spent about twenty-five years in Shelburne County. "I fell in love with the area," she told me when we talked in 1998. She surprised me by comparing her great-great-grandfather's seaside homeland to the once-simpler Ontario town of her childhood, the town he had founded: the mighty Oakville. "Shelburne today is as Oakville was, believe it or not, when I was in school," said Hart, "... population three thousand, and the lifestyle here is very much the same as during those years at Oakville."

She explained that, "you know everybody and you see everybody at the post office and you can walk to do your business up town. It's a very general feeling; the same as it was in Oakville, the small town," she said, sounding content.

It took two centuries, but that Chisholm clan came full circle, back to Nova Scotia. Just a few years ago, that circle closed forever. Nancy Hart also passed away, here at home.

NOVA SCOTIA'S DOUBLE OSCAR WINNER

Actor with no hands set a Hollywood record

And now please welcome the actor from Nova Scotia who set an all-time record at Hollywood's famous Academy Awards ceremony. He was awarded not one but two golden Oscar statuettes for the same movie role. Two for one! And it was a first. Plus, his performance in *The Best Years of Our Lives* was his first acting experience and, as a handicapped war veteran, he made his motion picture debut without hands. He was the amazing Harold Russell. In 2002 he passed away in his late eighties. But, my, what a life he had lived.

"I lost both my hands in an explosion when I was with the airborne troops," he told me in a telephone interview from Boston back in 1996. TNT exploded in his hands during training on June 6, 1944. Later, with hooks instead of hands, he appeared in an army training film.

"I was hospitalized in Washington DC," he said, "and they wanted to make a picture for rehabilitation purposes and I was the only bilateral amputee in the hospital and they picked me for the part."

That film led to his discovery. Hollywood director William Wyler decided to make the character of Homer Parrish in his movie a double amputee. Russell was given the part. *The Best Years of Our Lives* swept the Oscars of 1946. Russell won one Oscar for best supporting actor

RUSSELL: LOST BOTH HANDS BUT WON TWO OSCARS.

and was awarded a second "for bringing hope and courage to fellow veterans." A star was born.

Well, actually he was *born* in North Sydney, Nova Scotia. Russell was a young boy when his father died and his family moved from Cape Breton to Cambridge, Massachusetts in 1919. His first job was as a meat cutter. He attended Boston University and, after the war, was appointed by President Lyndon B. Johnson to a special committee on hiring the handicapped. He helped establish AMVETS, a viable alternative to the American Legion for veterans. He authored two autobiographies: *Victory In My Hands* and *The Best Years Of My Life*. He made rare acting appearances into his eighties, appearing in *Inside Moves* (1980) and *Dogtown* (1997) and in the TV show "China Beach."

However, this double Oscar winner had only one of his prized gold statuettes when we spoke. "I sold the other one for $62,000 dollars," he said. "I auctioned it off in New York."

"Why?" I asked, incredulous.

"I wanted some back-up cash," he said, "I didn't know what I was going to do. I was talking about a couple of businesses and so forth and it just seemed to be crazy to have two Oscars for something that happened years and years ago."

But he was downplaying his misfortune to me. Truth be told, Russell faced an ironic, American choice: Hollywood or health care. He had sold his valuable award to pay his wife's hefty medical bills.

The Academy of Motion Picture Arts and Sciences condemned the sale at the time. But Russell is quoted as saying, "I don't know why anybody would be critical. My wife's health is much more important than sentimental reasons. The movie will be here, even if Oscar isn't."

It was a noble act from a noble actor: selfless, loving, and humble. Proof, one might say, that this Nova Scotian Oscar winner was a star performer on the stage that really matters.

HINKY-DINKY PARLEZ-VOUS!

Did a soldier/songwriter from New Glasgow pen this classic war tune?

Mademoiselle from Armentieres, parlez-vous,
Mademoiselle from Armentieres, parlez-vous,
Mademoiselle from Armentieres,
She hasn't been kissed for forty years,
Hinky-dinky parlez-vous!

It's a classic, unmistakable, World War One marching song: "Mademoiselle from Armentieres." And the musician behind it was a soldier from New Glasgow. No kidding.

Lt. Gitz Rice, born Ingraham Rice (his brother nicknamed him as a toddler for the way he "gitz around"), has been given credit for this landmark singalong song, which is sometimes called "Hinky-Dinky Parlez-Vous."

Several old record albums I found attribute this song to Rice. His name is also linked with the "Mademoiselle" song on a list posted online by the American Society of Composers and Performers. And Edward Moogk, a former head of Sound Recording Selection with our National Library in Ottawa, writes in his book *Roll Back the Years* that this New Glasgow soldier created the "original adaptation" of "Mademoiselle from Armentieres."

Wake up! This is a local link to a musical milestone of the last century! Rice fought with the Canadian Expeditionary Force through many nasty World War One campaigns. Injured at Vimy Ridge in 1917, Rice then served as officer in charge of musical entertainment for 70,000 Canadian soldiers a week, according to *The Encyclopedia of Music in Canada.*

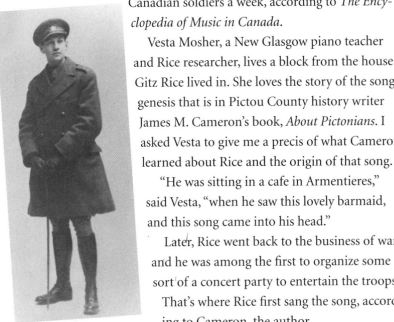

Vesta Mosher, a New Glasgow piano teacher and Rice researcher, lives a block from the house Gitz Rice lived in. She loves the story of the song's genesis that is in Pictou County history writer James M. Cameron's book, *About Pictonians.* I asked Vesta to give me a precis of what Cameron learned about Rice and the origin of that song.

"He was sitting in a cafe in Armentieres," said Vesta, "when he saw this lovely barmaid, and this song came into his head."

Later, Rice went back to the business of war and he was among the first to organize some sort of a concert party to entertain the troops.

That's where Rice first sang the song, according to Cameron, the author.

NEW GLASGOW'S RICE: "PARLAYED" HIS TUNE INTO A CLASSIC.

At least, that might be how it happened. Perhaps Rice wrote the first lyrics. But countless rude and ribald lyrics followed as soldiers added their own variations to the war tune. Some versions make it a downright dirty ditty.

One old record's liner notes explain that the real mademoiselle who inspired the song was purported to ply a fruit stall in the square in Armentieres, with special extra services offered behind a cloth screen. Hmmm, that was no lady, that was Mademoiselle from Armentieres.

This legendary tune gathered so many new lyrics, our National Library in Ottawa has a book (by the same name as the song) about the tune's history. That bit of scholarship also acknowledges Rice for his version of this song. That is, he either wrote some lyrics or he wrote or adapted the melody from somewhere.

Okay, so this ain't black and white. Nothing in war is easy. You see, there's evidence that bits of this marching (and drinking) tune evolved from lyrical fragments handed down more than 150 years ago by singing soldiers in other armies. So, perhaps from that tradition, Gitz Rice crafted the definitive version of this song; the one that we are all familiar with today.

"Is that your final answer?" you ask.

Nope. There's still this proviso: *The Encyclopedia of Music in Canada* says Rice's "authorship of the song is unsubstantiated." That doesn't mean he didn't or did write it. His adaptation of the old melody is perhaps more likely even though strong tradition has it that Rice was the song's creator.

Clear as mud? Well, all I can do is lay out the facts as I find them, contradictory or not. War is hell. But it seems fair to say Gitz Rice had a hand in popularizing and modernizing if not outright creating this snappy tune that's been performed and recorded by some of the world's greatest orchestras, brass bands, and vocalists.

Rice learned his music here at home, in Nova Scotia. James M. Cameron writes that Gitz Rice's father, a native of Bras d'Or, Cape Breton, settled in New Glasgow and became a well-known photographer and choirmaster who produced concerts around the province. Gitz played piano as a youngster. When the family moved to Montreal, he studied at the McGill conservatory. He and his brother became entertainers.

Post-war, Rice did vaudeville shows and even entertained our troops during World War Two. His other big hit was "Dear Old Pal of Mine." Rice also wrote "Some Day I'll Come Back to You", "On the Road That Leads Back Home," "We Stopped Them At the Marne," and many other songs. He produced two recordings: the ironically titled "Fun in Flanders," and "Life in a Trench in Belgium."

In 1947, Gitz Rice died in New York. His recorded music is stored as a Canadian treasure in our National Library in Ottawa.

CAPE BRETON LULLABY

The McCarthy-era rebel who penned our pretty, pastoral tune

Driftwood is burning blue, wild walk the wall shadows
Night winds go riding by, riding by the lochie meadows
On to the break of day, close Mira stream singing:
Caidil gu latha laddie, latha laddie. *Sleep the dark away.*

Close by Beinn Bhreagh's stream, wander the lost lambies
Here, there and everywhere, everywhere their troubled mammies
Find them and bring them home, sing them to sleep singing:
Caidil gu latha laddie, latha laddie. *Sleep the night away.*

Daddy is on the bay, he'll keep a pot brewin'
Save us from tumbling down, tumbling down to rack and ruin
Pray Mary send him home, safe from the foam singing:
Caidil gu latha laddie, latha laddie. *Sleep the stars away.*

Recorded by many maritime artists, the lovely song "Cape Breton Lullaby" offers a soft, romantic view of the island's traditional way of life. But its author, Kenneth Leslie, was, in contrast, a modern radical journalist in New York. He was a social activist, a rebel, and a theological philosopher. *Life* magazine listed him with the likes of Albert Einstein, Thomas Mann, and Charlie Chaplin as leftists to keep a suspicious eye on in the era of Senator Joseph McCarthy's paranoid communist witch hunt. Leslie was also known for having won Canada's Governor General's Award for his poetry. He cherished his Nova Scotian Scottish heritage.

LESLIE: LULLABY LYRICS BY A LEFTIST!

Born in 1892 in Pictou, and educated at Dalhousie in Halifax, Leslie did graduate work in philosophy and mysticism at Harvard University. In the 1920s, he founded the Song Fishermen, a sort of literary Group of Seven made up of Maritime poets and journalists such as: Charles G. D. Roberts, Charles Bruce, Robert Norwood and Bliss Carmen. Their mimeographed sheets of Maritime and socially conscious poetry went out across North America.

"These were not writers that had misty eyes about reality," said Dr. Gwenn Davies, of the University of New Brunswick.

"On one level, they celebrated the beauty and the cultural traditions of Nova Scotia," she said, "and at the same time, they knew a lot of the social realities: the poverty, the out migration and so on."

One member of the Song Fishermen, Andrew Merkel, for example, "might have written very romantic poems about the sea but at the same time, as a reporter, he was covering the strikes in the 1920s in the mines in Cape Breton."

Leslie's writings were similarly mixed. He celebrated the hardworking Maritime fisherman in his poetry while also condemning racial segregation and anti-Semitism in America. His poem "O'Malley to the Reds" was inspired by Father Moses Coady's famous Antigonish Movement of self help and rural co-operativism.

"Leslie was an anti-imperialist, Christian socialist," said Dr. David Latham from his office at Toronto's York University. "He wanted to free the Maritimes from exploitation by powerful companies."

This Pictou poet founded the radical *Protestant Digest* magazine in 1938 and published it in New York. He gathered a board of major thinkers, some of them German refugees from Adolf Hitler's increasingly restrictive world. "He was trying to make people aware of some terrible things that were starting to happen in Germany," said Dr. Davies from her UNB office in Fredericton.

Later, Leslie's writings also showed "concern that Hitlerite views were arising in Britain and in America." His poem "Remember Lamumba" spoke up for the black cause in Africa. Leslie's world concern ran wide and deep.

When the McCarthyites asked for a copy of the subscription list to Leslie's leftist magazine, he refused. "And he was named by *Life* magazine as what was called a 'fellow traveller,'" said Davies. At that point, Leslie returned to Nova Scotia. Editing *The Protestant* from here until 1953, Leslie continued writing into his eighties, putting out smaller publications called *Man* and *New Man* between 1957 and 1972.

"He just kept expressing his concern about the threat of war, about the impact of American imperialism," said Davies.

It was back here, in his home province, that he wrote "some of his most socially articulate poetry about the state of the world." He also wrote "Halibut Cove Harvest," a prophetic poem about individual fishermen "reaping" from the sea while big corporate fishing vessels were "raping" the sea.

As high-minded as this heavy thinker was, he had a deep affinity for the simple pleasures of the Celtic culture of his homeland. He played the fiddle. His first wife—a Moir of the wealthy Halifax candy merchant family—played piano. Their daughters step danced. Leslie had promoted this Scottish heritage on a radio broadcast he ran out of New York. The Leslie family visited Cape Breton where they socialized with the well-to-do Grosvenors, Alexander Bell's in-laws who founded *National Geographic*.

This philosopher poet from Pictou passed away in a Halifax seniors' home in 1974. He was 82.

Chuck Lapp, a Halifax documentary maker, was working on a biographical portrait of Leslie for Vision TV when I interviewed him about this amazing Nova Scotian. And what a varied portrait! Kenneth Leslie was a stout-hearted Christian socialist, prolific leftist journalist, and... a lullaby writer!

REVEREND WHITE'S REMARKABLE COINCIDENCE

After many black breakthroughs, two amazing reunions

F rom slavery to highest honours; from so-called Virginian coloured boy, he gained the respected titles of Reverend, Doctor and
Captain. He was William Andrew White, a highly regarded Baptist
minister in Nova Scotia, the first black preacher on radio in Canada
(on CHNS Radio in Halifax), and the first black officer in the British
Commonwealth. All this, over sixty years ago. But there's a newly discovered, modern-day twist to this preacher's inspiring life story.

The father of Nova Scotia's internationally famous contralto singer,
Portia White, Rev. White was born in 1874 and rose from a family that
was enslaved in Virginia.

Helena Blackadar, a Nova Scotian teacher living in the south, told
him about Wolfville's Acadia University, where White later became only
the second black graduate, in 1903.

A skilled athlete, White was almost banned from a Halifax rugby
field by the racist coach of an opposing university team. But Acadia's
coach backed White. The game went on. According to Lorne White,
Rev. White's son and Portia's brother, who still lives in the Halifax area,

that coach's support changed Rev. White's life forever.

"He told Portia later," said Lorne White, "that one of the reasons he stayed in Canada was that he realized they look on the inside of a man, not the outside, and he chose to raise his family here."

Rev. White founded a Baptist church in New Glasgow and later served a congregation in Truro, where daughter Portia was born. Finally settling in Halifax, he engaged in bold pulpit exchanges: black and white ministers preaching at each other's churches. Segregationists must have cringed.

But when White donned a uniform to go serve his country, the race issue pursued him. Canada's No. 2 Construction Battalion, a unique all-black unit, joined the Great War with Capt. Rev. White leading the men as their chaplain. Based in France, these black soldiers were permitted tools but not rifles. They cut the lumber for bridges, spread barbed wire, and dug trenches; the labour of war.

The only medical officer willing to treat the overworked, exhausted black soldiers was a "colour blind" physician, Dr. Dan Murray. He and Rev. White bonded, becoming wartime buddies. White's war diary and Murray's hundreds of letters home each mention the other man many times.

"Like, 'Capt. White and I today went to a wrestling match' or 'Dr. Murray and I went over to visit some friends,' that kind of thing," said Lorne White, quoting the old writings as we talked at his home in Halifax in 2002. So, it's clear that the man of the cloth and the good doctor became fond friends in a time of war, more than eighty years ago.

But remember that modern-day twist to the story that I promised? It was Canadian actor and filmmaker Anthony Sherwood, a relative of the Whites, who discovered something interesting about that doctor's identity. His discovery uncovered a remarkable coincidence and led to a wonderful reunion of sorts.

Sherwood's docudrama, *Honour Before Glory*, unveils that Dr. Murray was the grandfather of Anne Murray, the famous singer from Springhill, Nova Scotia. Why is that so cool? Well, Lorne White—also a singer—was certainly surprised by that news. Actually, he was bowled over by it. "I said, 'Are you kidding?'" said Lorne, recalling his chat with the filmmaker. "Because Anne Murray and I had been on Singalong Jubilee," said Lorne White, referring to the 1960s CBC TV show on which he also sang. "And we had no idea what that relationship was between the two families!"

"It was really quite exciting when we discovered that Dr. Murray had written four hundred letters home to his wife and Anne's brother, Bruce Murray, has all the letters," he said.

When Sherwood, the filmmaker, compared the doctor's letters to the entries in Rev. White's diaries, "they were identical!"

These wartime friends passed away, not knowing that a descendant from each of them would one day perform side by side on national TV. In fact, no one knew until Sherwood's modern-day docudrama was made. The film includes the reunion between the famous recording artist Anne Murray and her one-time fellow TV singer, Lorne White. The camera is rolling as the two meet for the first time since learning of this strange but special discovery; that her grandfather and

REV. WHITE: A WORLD WAR ONE–
ANNE MURRAY CONNECTION.

his father helped each other endure the loneliness, labour, and even the racism of wartime service in France during World War One. Anne and Lorne laugh, reminisce about their days performing together, and share in their mutual amazement over this family connection about which they never knew when they appeared together in front of the TV camera some forty years earlier. The story had come full circle for them and it was nice to see.

Rev. White's story also included a very poignant completion for him. Just before he died, in 1936, Rev. White received an unprecedented honour for a black man in Canada: an honourary degree from his alma mater. He became the Reverend Doctor William Andrew White. He was also given a chauffeured drive back to his old childhood homeland of King and Queen County, Virginia. White and his wife Izie and their not-yet-famous daughter, Portia, drove—as if back in time—down to the American South. White walked the land his parents and siblings had literally slaved upon.

But he was very sick during that trip south. Many thought the cancer would claim White before he could return home. He asked that, if he died, he be buried back in Nova Scotia.

Addressing a crowd of the extended White family in a small Virginian church, the dying preacher was warmly greeted. His overdue return to his old homeland had strengthened his already positive spirit as he spoke.

"He told them how, as a result of being there, he had improved to a degree," said Lorne White.

"I guess just being home meant so much to him; just to go down and have a last look at his beginnings, you know?"

He had truly come full circle. But it was his chosen homeland where he wanted the circle to finally close.

The gravely ill preacher barely survived the long drive back to Nova Scotia. He died just days later. The Cornwallis Street Baptist Church in Halifax was packed to the walls with the biggest funeral service Halifax had ever seen. The street was filled, sidewalk to sidewalk, with a throng of mourners walking behind the casket procession.

This son of slaves who rose to such heights in his Nova Scotian home was absolutely admired and deeply loved. And, even now, still missed.

AN AFRICAN
GOLD-MINING MYSTERY

Did this Cape Breton prospector strike it rich before being shot?

R obert Mugabe's Zimbabwe is a troubled country these days, as it was in 1896 when, on its way to being known as Rhodesia, the region saw natives at war with white gold miners. Caught in the furor of flying bullets, a lone Nova Scotian prospector died where he had staked his claim. But almost six decades passed before his family in North Sydney even heard of his fate. They've wondered since if he perhaps left behind any riches.

Charles Annesty was mining his own, small, independent stake close to the big Alice Mine in southeastern Africa. He was working separately from Cecil Rhodes—of the famous Rhodes Scholarships fame—whose British South Africa Company had claimed that gold-rich territory against the native peoples' wishes.

After his wife died, Annesty left his infant daughter, Rita May, with a family in Cape Breton and joined Canada's North West Mounted Police before going to seek his fortune in Africa.

When she was about thirteen, his daughter apparently heard that the father she never knew was missing. But it wasn't until she was a woman in her seventies, back in the 1960s, that she finally learned of his tragic fate. Her son, Cliff Gallop, seventy-five, of North Sydney, has been holding on to a package of documents sent to the family forty years ago that explains what happened to his grandfather, the missing gold prospector. It's an old family story of death and discovery.

One document is written by A. S. Hickman, apparently a Rhodesian historian, describing how a gold prospector in the 1950s was working Charles Annesty's original 1896 claim and found human bones near a gold "reef."

"In 1957, in the valley below the mine shaft," writes Hickman, "he was using a bulldozer to expose the reef when his employees reported the finding of a human skeleton." The remains were not far from the Alice Mine.

Archaeologists studied the bones. The find was written up in the 1962 *Central African Journal of Medicine* (see illustration p. 162) and a *Rhodesian Herald* reporter inspected the discovery. The remains were assumed to be those of Annesty: the last missing man to be identified after the infamous 1896 uprising of the maShona—or Shona—people.

"They discovered that he was shot, but there was an awful lot of people shot at the same time and they didn't find my grandfather's body," said Gallop.

Sometime in the 1960s, Hickman, the historian, contacted Mr. Gallop's mother—Annesty's daughter—in North Sydney. He had somehow traced the serial number on a metal water canteen found amid the miner's remains to the RCMP in Ottawa, who identified him as a former member of their force and directed the historian to the family.

Since then, they've occasionally wondered if Annesty had left them any gold. "We often did joke about it," said Gallop. "We should have gone over but we had no idea where he was or what happened to him."

It was one of the last remaining mysteries of the bloody Shona uprising and Charles Annesty's name is part of that history.

"I have seen his name come up in Rhodesianna," said Professor Tim Burke of Swarthmore College in Pennsylvania. Burke has been a Rhodesian history scholar for ten years and agreed to answer my inquiries when I reached him by phone.

"He [Annesty] was always assumed to be a casualty [of the uprising]," said Burke. "He was listed in the lists of the dead because he went missing."

Other British miners and their wives sought the protection of the Alice Mine but it seems Annesty didn't make it.

The Shona were joined by the Ndebele tribe in the attack. The white workers in the mine held them off by shooting guns and throwing miners' dynamite sticks until the armed Mazowe Patrol arrived to get them out. A small wagon was reinforced with bulletproof metal sheeting and the British civilians were loaded in and taken through a gauntlet of a thousand uprising attackers in the valley, to the town then called Salisbury.

"They fought their way in through a cordon, a sieging force of Shona warriors," said Professor Burke, "and lost, I think, three men and five were wounded....Some of the miners in the area had been killed before they got to the Alice Mine." Annesty was on his own in that clash of cultures. Ironically, Burke said the independent prospectors like Annesty usually had good relations with the natives, based on trade.

But he didn't make it out alive. He likely never struck it rich either. Reaching the deep gold seam in that reef traditionally required hefty equipment and plenty of funding. Mr. Rhodes's company had both those things at the Alice Mine, but the nearby independent prospectors working the same seam were on more of a shoestring budget.

"Most of the minerals that could be mined out of it were not ones that could be mined by individual miners on individual stakes," said Burke.

Today, Cliff Gallop can boast of no shiny nugget inheritance, but he has had for many years this gem of an old family story to treasure and to pass on to his grandchildren. And yet, naturally, he still wonders if his grandfather maybe left behind a stash of gold—somewhere—for future generations to find. Wouldn't you wonder too?

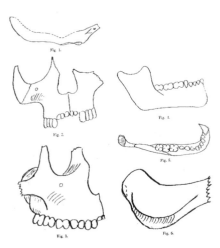

KILLED IN AFRICA: A CAPE BRETON MINER'S REMAINS.

STAIRS AND ROPES!

Clever captains of commerce built Dartmouth's historic Ropeworks

Hauling away on ropes and rigging is part of the birth story of this sea-bound province. But here's a twist: It wasn't all done at sea. Picture a wooden building almost four hundred metres (a quarter mile) long where hemp from all over the world was spun and stretched to the lengths required by tall ships and schooners. That ropewalk building was part of Dartmouth Ropeworks, a huge factory that stood on the east side of Halifax harbour. Part of its complex still stands as a well-known Dartmouth watering hole called the Old Mill Tavern.

That part of Dartmouth, just north of the present-day Macdonald Bridge, was almost an independent company town during the late 1800s. The factory was its centre, built by the prominent Stairs family of the William Stairs, Son and Morrow ship chandlery business on Water Street in Halifax.

I poked around the old Dartmouth Ropeworks neighbourhood with Jim Frost, a marine business consultant who's researched the Stairs family.

"They had the factory that employed at least three hundred people," said Frost. "There were at least one hundred company houses, so the whole north end of Dartmouth grew up around Dartmouth Ropeworks."

Frost's Ropeworks research is contained in the book *Industry and Society in Nova Scotia*, published in 2001. He has also researched the Stairs family itself for his book *Merchant Princes* (2003).

He pointed out the Stairs United Church on Hester Street, which he said evolved from the community centre the Stairs had built for its workers. They also benevolently held a hundred or so mortgages for their employees. On many streets—John and George for example (named for Stairs family members, not Beatles)—there are rows of century-old company houses built for workers at Dartmouth Ropeworks.

The Old Mill Tavern building on Wyse Road was a key part of the old factory. Frost and I went there to investigate, strictly for research purposes of course. The tavern's large foundation stones and thick-hewn wooden beams inside hint at its age. The remaining part of the long ropewalk was attached to the back of the tavern. At least it was the day we toured through it.

The ropewalk was a narrow wooden warehouse with a high ceiling. Weak floorboards were worn, one might imagine, by decades of weary rope-hauling factory workers treading its length.

"That ropewalk went back about four hundred metres from Wyse Road," said Frost. "They basically walked the strings of hemp out to the end of the rope, so to speak. That's how they made hawsers," he said, referring to very thick ropes used to tie large vessels to a wharf.

The raw hemp was sailed into the harbour, offloaded at the Stairs's wharf, carted up the hill to the Ropeworks and spun and pulled into ropes of all lengths and widths. A rope remnant as thick as a tree trunk—a hawser—is kept at the Dartmouth Heritage Museum. Unfortunately, the long ropewalk building we had toured burned down in a spectacular fire a week later. Only the tavern part remains.

The Stairs ropes sold internationally. But as the age of wooden ships passed, the call for marine ropes diminished. Something had to be done. Originally staunchly anti-Confederation, the Stairs clan changed their position to support John A. Macdonald's country-building quest. They looked to the new railway to help them in their future ropemaking ways. It was a common gamble of the day. Could Nova Scotia advance by turning its back on overseas markets and trading inland, thereby strengthening the new country, Canada?

Even today, some will say that was our economic downfall. But in the case of entrepreneur William J. Stairs, the plan worked. Nearly sixty years old at the time, he lead a company group on a long, rugged business journey into Canada's west.

He travelled "by train, by boat, and eventually by horseback, camping under the stars."

"They came back and ordered machinery to make binder twine," said Frost, "and eventually captured a third of the Canadian market, making binder twine, which the farmers in the west used to bind the hay sheaves."

"They made that stuff right here in Dartmouth," said Frost.

Their reduced marine rope business also continued, but with a new nautical adaptation.

"When the fishery started to develop in the 1890s and the turn of the last century," said Frost, "the Stairs started to make smaller, fishing rope. Rather than bemoan the past and the demise of the sailing ship, they were able to adjust their business to changing circumstances."

Ropemakers flexible enough to get out of a bind? Punful but true. However, when the government got federal prisons into rope manufacturing, John F. Stairs, the MP for Halifax at that stage, had to fight a lonely battle against it.

The Stairs were business survivors. They eventually lead a national merger of Canadian rope producers, creating Consumers Cordage, a company controlled and managed in Dartmouth until the 1930s. They sold out in 1938 to Plymouth Cordage of Massachusetts. But one Cyril Stairs sat on that American firm's board, maintaining the family's ties to rope.

By 1956 synthetic ropes and cheaper overseas competition finally ended the Stairs family's long association with rope manufacturing; a run which lasted nearly ninety years. That's a lot of rope this Nova Scotian company sent out on the seven seas. These captains of business gave us the ties that bind us to the nautical heritage of the age of sail around the world.

DARTMOUTH'S ROPE WENT AROUND THE WORLD.

A LONG ROW HOME

Seven fishermen survive a sinking, hundreds of miles out

I n the lovely fishing village of Sambro, not far from Halifax, I was smiling in awe when I met this veteran swordfisherman on his wharf. At eighty-seven years old, Harold Henneberry's sturdy frame still allowed him to go to sea, harpooning—or "stickin'"—the big fish from the bow of the boat. The ocean was his life, in good times and bad. Sometimes the job called for a strong arm, sometimes strong leadership ability. Harold had both. Rugged, cheery, and optimistic, he sat in the sun on a wooden fish box that day and recalled for me the time he once helped save his crew of six men, as his boat sank about 400 kilometres (250 miles) off Newfoundland.

It was 1956. Harold and six buddies were on his twenty-six metre (eighty-six foot) vessel, the *Angela B. Mills*, on the tail of the Grand Banks.

Hurricane Betsy blew up the coast from New England. To let her blast by, they sailed farther out. But soon after, trouble struck in the dead of night.

"One fella come back and yelled, 'We're sinkin'!" said Harold. A leak had sprung. He remembered the scene vividly. "When we looked down in the engine room, just the top of the engine was out of the water."

The ocean was flowing in. "In the fo'c'sle, the water was washing the boots around and we knew we were sinkin'," he said. "We got the pump going but the water was too high to run it off the main engine; everything stopped and the water was starting to creep up."

While his crew launched the wooden dories, Harold boldly stepped down into the rapidly flooding belowdecks.

"The vessel was going down then; about half of it was under water," he said. "The stern was sticking up; we got down forward and got a few canned goods underneath the water but it was up around our neck then."

In traditional Maritimer-speak, he described the dynamics of the disaster. "Every time the boat would heave, it would throw you off your feet, when she give a heave," he said.

He grabbed only essentials: canned food, bread loaves and about ten bottles of whisky.

The radio wasn't working. Outside, one dory loaded with supplies was crushed under the sinking vessel. The men in the other dories yelled at Harold to get off the doomed fishing boat, but he went back inside for the compass and a hand-cranked signal horn.

Soon, all seven fishermen were aboard three wooden dories, roped together in the vast empty ocean. They had no rescue suits or electronic signalling equipment back then. Just seven rowers. So they rowed and rested and rowed, day and night; soaked to the skin, with little food in cold rain and biting sea spray.

"We had an old blanket we'd hold out over the stern of the dory and the sea would hit you in the back and the blanket would throw the water off," he said.

"Then we'd bail the rest out. We done that all night, one night." Their collected rain water was mixed with salt water. They drank it anyway.

They were drenched, shivering, and sore with no relief in sight. One morning, the youngest of the men was face down in the bow, wasted and giving up. Harold propped him up, put the oars back in his hands, and in a few minutes, the exhausted man was rowing again. Harold shot a seabird. "We ate it raw," he said. "We had to, we were starving."

They washed it down with the booze. "Every now and then we'd take a small sip of whisky," said Harold. "Not very much, we didn't want to get drunk. That kept us going I believe; it was so cold, we were soaking wet," he said. "A couple nights it couldn't rain any harder—it just squeezed us down in the dory."

Seven men lasted seven days, rowing and bailing water continuously. Two ships and a search plane passed without seeing them. Harold thought of nailing his wallet to the side of the dory—in case he didn't make it. But he didn't want to discourage the men. He knew they wouldn't last one more night. Then, he saw something. Standing up, he looked north. "I said, 'Look! That's land!'"

He knew that the distant, shiny, fine weather clouds meant land ho! The men thought he was crazy and yelled the same but "sure enough it was the closest land we could have made!"

"Then the fellers, they got life in them then," said Harold, grinning somewhat toothlessly at the memory. "They seen land, then they took to rowin'!"

I'll bet they did.

Some cried out, "We're going to make it!" They broke out a final quart of whisky. A Newfoundland fisherman picked them up just in time and took them in to Trepassey. They were very weak, their flesh raw and oozing in spots. But they were alive. Back in Sambro, Nova Scotia, where Harold's wife Geraldine was frantic, alone with four children, she had a dream that a man entered her driveway yelling, "They're found!"

It was a Sunday evening when her dream came true. Geraldine heard church bells and car horns in the village as a local man entered her driveway yelling, "They're found, they're found!"

"I said, 'I don't believe it, those were the words that I heard in my dream,'" said Geraldine.

"That brought it all back then," she said.

Harold arrived home in bad shape. With time, he recovered and chose to return to the hazardous life of a fisherman. In 2001, forty-five years after that terrible row home, Harold chuckled and told me he was still going out to help out swordfishing crews once in a while. He said he just loved being out there. And in the summer of 2003, at almost ninety years old, he was out there again. The old fisherman has never tired of the life at sea, even after the sea almost claimed his life.

THE *SALADIN* MUTINY

A saga of death, deception, and a Halifax hanging

A mysterious carved figurehead of a turban-wearing Turk, long preserved in Halifax, is a reminder of a less-than-nostalgic tale from our nautical past.

The one-and-a-quarter-metre (four-feet) high figure of a bushy-browed man with piercing eyes is allegedly from the prow of the vessel *Saladin*. In 1844, her crew's brutal and foolish acts of piracy lead to a sensational trial and public hanging in Halifax.

Today, this odd figurehead sits at the Maritime Museum of the Atlantic in Halifax. It once sat nearby, in the offices of William Stairs, Son and Morrow Ltd., a ship chandlery on Sackville Street. A reproduction of this figurehead was mounted over the front door of the old Stairs house, now a Dalhousie University campus building on Halifax's South Street.

If this fierce-looking guy was in fact once mounted on *Saladin*'s bow, what a tragic tale he could tell.

The scene on the ship was gruesome. Bloody axes, dead bodies, murderous sailors enraged and drunk. The wooden barque *Saladin* was sailing from Chile for England, loaded with pure silver coins and other cargo.

Captain Sandy MacKenzie was among fourteen or so on board, including another captain, George Fielding, a shady, unsavory type, just catching a ride to England. Or so he said. Out on the Atlantic, encouraged by alcohol and by Fielding's lead, *Saladin*'s crew launched into a bloody mutiny. Eight people on board were brutally attacked and killed, including the ship's captain, MacKenzie. The confession of one of the mutineers, named Jones, was later recorded in trial transcripts:

"I took hold of his hands and Fielding struck him two blows with the axe…Fielding hauled him forward in front of the companion and struck him again and then threw him overboard. Then Fielding, Hazelton, Anderson, and Johnson went down to take some liquor and said, 'The vessel is now our own!'"

But there's no honour among thieves, especially mutinous, pirating thieves.

Dr. David Flemming, past director of the Maritime Museum of the Atlantic in Halifax, described to me how the suspicious sailors then turned on their own leader in the mutiny. "The other mutineers were a bit worried about Fielding," he said. "They thought he was getting cold feet. They decided they should dispose of him as well."

And they did. By then, the young crew, in a well-liquored haze, realized they had murdered the most skilled navigators on board: two captains and the first mate.

"They really hadn't given it much thought, I guess," said Flemming.

The *Saladin* hit the rocks in full sail off the shore of Guysborough County, Nova Scotia.

A third ship's master, Captain Cunningham of the schooner *Billow* arrived on the scene and was hoisted on board *Saladin* to offer help. He didn't swallow the drunken crew's lies about their captain falling overboard and other sailors taking sick and dying. He knew something was up. Captain Cunningham alerted the authorities in Halifax.

Four mutineers—Jones, Hazelton, Anderson, and Trevaskiss (alias Johnson)—were tried for piracy and murder. Two others were tried for murder. News of their impending hanging was widely published in two major Nova Scotian newspapers of the day: the *Morning Post* and the *Acadian Recorder*.

The gallows was erected in Halifax, near the present-day hospital building known as the Victoria General. Entire families gathered in the hot sun. Soldiers circled the platform. Clergymen knelt in prayer.

The condemned exchanged parting words. The prisoner, Jones,

kissed his fellow comrades affectionately on the cheeks. He told the crowd he was sorry and publicly asked for God's forgiveness. Caps were pulled over the prisoners' heads. The ropes were adjusted. These misguided sailors were publicly executed June 30, 1844. Not one of them was over the age of twenty-three.

The reproduction of *Saladin*'s alleged figurehead is still there on the old Stairs house at 6230 South Street in Halifax. You can see this reminder of inhumane savagery fastened above the front door of the building which now houses Dalhousie's School of Health and Human Performance.

It seems, years ago, someone considered it wiser to put a reproduction on display there, deeming the original worth protecting. Good thing. The duplicate figurehead over the doorway was beheaded by student pranksters. I'm told that one year the head was replaced by a pumpkin. I'm guessing the vandals were not students of history. If they were, they might have realized the *Saladin* saga is nothing to joke about. It was a gruesome tragedy that permanently scarred Nova Scotia's nautical heritage; a mindless, bloody event that shook the city when it happened and stayed in Haligonians' collective memory for many, many years following.

SIDEBURNS AND ASSASSINATION

Our theatrical link to Lincoln and Elvis

Would you believe the fellow who made mutton-chop sideburns famous and fashionable ran an early theatre in Nova Scotia's capital city? You heard it here first. I guess Elvis Presley owes him one.

His name was Edward Askew Sothern, best known for his widely popular interpretation of the quirky Lord Dundreary character in the historic play *Our American Cousin,* by playwright Tom Taylor. Sothern partially crafted that famous Dundreary character in Halifax after arriving from New York to gain acting and theatre managing experience.

He set up his drama house in an old hay barn 150 years ago. The Theatre at Spring Gardens—also known as the Theatre Royal and later as Sothern's Lyceum—sat near the northwest corner of Halifax's Spring Garden Road and Queen Street intersection, beside the present Back Pages used book store.

Garrison men had used the building initially for amateur theatrical performances. But Sothern took it over, renovated it to seat about seven hundred, and brought famous American actors onto its stage.

Mostly, it was a tough go for Sothern's stage in a barn. Theatre troupes came and went. Sothern did his best to make a profit. One time, he narrowly escaped being thrown into debtor's prison in Halifax.

But he wisely had invited some big stars of the American stage to draw a big enough crowd that season to cover his costs. Another time, the Halifax firemen sponsored an evening to bail out Sothern's drama barn. Still, the Theatre at Spring Gardens had its flaws.

"The curtain in front of the stage scarcely reached the stage floor," said Dr. Alan Andrews, a teacher of theatre at Dalhousie University. We sat across from the old theatre site on Queen, talking about old newspaper accounts Andrews has read about Sothern's venture. "With the doors opened, the wind would blow so that you could actually see behind the curtain after it had supposedly come down to conceal all of that!"

Oops.

Needless to say, it was a struggle for Sothern during his three years here. Yet, some shows drew healthy crowds and very good press in the old Halifax newspapers. Being close, by sea, to the big cities, Halifax was on the theatre circuit and many great plays came to be performed in Sothern's old barn theatre.

"There was a kind of Broadway-in-your-own-backyard formula that he used," said Andrews.

"Citizens of Halifax welcomed it," he said, "these were plays that people in New York or in London had only recently seen for the first time so it gave them the feeling they were part of a larger culture."

Sothern was ambitious to make it to the top in theatre, somewhere. He really put his mark on the character of the stupid aristocrat, Lord Dundreary. His Dundreary always drew appreciative audiences and stole the show.

"Probably after he left Halifax, Sothern realized he could do something with the character of Lord Dundreary," said Andrews.

"He slowly added business and dialogue to the character so that Dundreary became *the* reason to go and see the play."

The Dundreary image slipped from stage into greater society in the 1850s and 1860s. Just like trendy, modern-day Hollywood spinoffs.

"He turned Dundreary into a character of such fame that the whiskers he wore in the role, sometimes called mutton-chop whiskers, came to be known as Dundreary whiskers," said Andrews.

"And parts of his costume, a scarf for example, came to be known as a Dundreary scarf and people would wear this," he said.

Popular on- and off-stage, Sothern began doing Dundreary spinoffs: new storylines written specifically for that character. This creative thievery was of course before copyright laws.

His outlandish, sideburned character became known internationally, from Halifax to London to Washington. Even when other actors played the role, it was Sothern's mark on the character that drew the crowds to *Our American Cousin*. It also drew an American leader to his death.

"By the 1860s this had become a play that everybody wanted to see," said Andrews.

In 1865, it was on stage at the Ford's Theatre in Washington. Can you guess what's coming?

"Abraham Lincoln had obviously decided that its reputation deserved his attention," said Andrews," so he was there that night to see the play."

Lincoln was assassinated that night.

A tenuous tether from Halifax to Lincoln's death, but it's our dubious link to claim if we want to.

Eventually, the experience Sothern gained in Nova Scotia and elsewhere did get him to the big time. He became theatre manager in England, at the distinguished Haymarket Theatre.

A big step up from Halifax's hay barn theatre!

SOTHERN AS LORD DUNDREARY:
SENSATIONAL SIDEBURNS AND
OUR LINK TO LINCOLN!

SWASTIKAS AT OUR CENTRE OF POWER

The evil Nazi emblem crops up in odd places in Nova Scotia

What did Nazi Germany and Nova Scotia have in common? Each had the swastika symbol posted at its centre of power. This province still does. But in our case, the power centre is just that, a big hydro-electric generator at St. Margaret's Bay, near Halifax. Just like the one at Black River, the huge cast metal equipment there bears a plaque showing the manufacturer's name—ASEA—with a swastika, like a company logo, beside it.

Nova Scotia Power tells me ASEA was the Swedish General Electric. It later merged with the international corporation, Siemens. So why did a Swedish company put the evil Nazi symbol on its products?

To answer that, let me introduce another oddly placed swastika in our provincial past. In Garth Vaughan's book, *The Puck Starts Here*, I see that Windsor, the alleged birthplace of hockey, once had a hockey team called the Swastikas with the four-legged, spiraling symbol we associate with Adolf Hitler on their hockey sweaters.

Jim Wilcox, a nephew of Blaine Sexton, the Swastika's star player, realizes the team photo is shocking to the uninitiated. "We hate the swastika," said the eighty-something Windsor man, "because we went through a very bad war with the Germans and that was their main emblem." But "the swastika is a good-luck emblem from way back and of course these guys were looking for good luck in their hockey so I suppose that's where the name Windsor Swastikas came from."

Good luck? Hmmm. Even this Know-It-All didn't know!

So I sought out a swastika expert. I called an artist in Cranbrook, British Columbia, who has a museum to the symbol in his house and is writing a book on the symbol's past, called *Gentle Swastika*. No kidding!

His name is as eccentric as his hobby. He had it legally changed to the all-inclusive ManWoman (No, I am not making this up! Check his swastika website at http://www.ManWoman.net/swastika/). Well studied in swastika history, Mr.—or Ms.—ManWoman explained to me that the word comes from ancient sanskrit and means "to be of good fortune."

"It was very common as a good luck sign," said ManWoman. "It goes back 5,000–10,000 thousand years. It has a long and very vast history around the world."

He suggested psychologist Karl Jung would explain the worldwide variation on the swastika theme as proof of a collective unconscious. "It shows up everywhere," he said.

The shapes vary. Some are "curved and sometimes backwards and sometimes they've got five legs or three legs." Others have "little hooks or little feet on the end."

Native North Americans used the symbol. (I'm told the Mic Mac Aquatic Club in Dartmouth removed its swastika from its building exterior when war broke out.)

"I've got examples from the Haida, Cree, Navaho, Hopi and the Kickaboos," said the BC swastika researcher.

HITLER'S HOCKEY TEAM? NOPE, GUESS AGAIN!

All the ancient peoples drew swastikas: "Romans, Greeks, Etruscans, Vikings. There's hardly a place that you can't find it in the orient," he said, "because of Buddhism and Hinduism; it is actually one of their sacred symbols."

Perhaps you've seen swastikas as good-luck pendants or in mosaic designs of some church floors.

There's a 1931 Newfoundland stamp honouring pioneer airplane flights with swastikas in the stamp's corners.

And, just like in Nova Scotia, there were two western hockey teams—girls' teams—called the Swastikas in the 1916–1920s era.

Nazi Germany simply propagandized an ancient, multicultural emblem of good luck.

"The German dentist who designed the flag for Hitler actually put a swavastika, the backwards swastika on the flag," said my B.C. swastika researcher.

That's the one that points to the left.

"Hitler didn't want any part of that because left is communism and right is fascism," he said.

So the Nazi swastika pointed right and was tilted to the right, up on one corner.

Therefore, don't panic. Nova Scotia Power's hydro equipment is marked for luck, not world domination.

Though, given their present price per kilowatt hour, I'm not so sure! To their lawyers: that was a joke.

Postscript: Some time after telling the above story on CBC Radio, I checked again with Nova Scotia Power. A helpful public relations person had sent me a digital picture of the swastika on their equipment, but this time I wanted to go see it, accompanied by a TV camera. The PR person must have been replaced by someone a bit more concerned with protecting the corporation's image. By the time the new media relations person responded to my request for a swastika visit, she was able to report that unfortunately the metal symbol had been removed from that equipment. Ah well, it's understandable that the old symbol still makes people nervous. It's just too bad more of us aren't aware of its original meaning.

TARZAN MEETS PRINCE VALIANT IN NOVA SCOTIA!

Our link to the world's greatest comic book heroes

Long before I was leaping from piano top onto the basement couch with my apeman's yell at full volume, Tarzan had captured other kids' imaginations too. I watched the television series, read the comic books and, later, saw the movies. But the image of the loin-clothed jungle man first reached a worldwide audience in those colourful, syndicated, Sunday newspaper comic strips. The artist who created the Tarzan strip was born and raised in Nova Scotia.

He was one of the great pioneers of classic comic strip art, back when formal, realistic illustration and storytelling ruled the funny papers; pre-Dilbert. His narrative strips remained popular for decades. He was Hal Foster—Harold Rudolph Foster—born in Halifax on August 16, 1892.

Edgar Rice Burroughs's Tarzan character was Foster's foray into comic strip art in 1929. A meticulous craftsman, Foster even edited some of the Tarzan storylines.

At Strange Adventures, a Halifax comic book store, I learned that an original Foster today is worth over $5,000.

"The depictions he made really grew to become the standard for a lot of people; the Hal Foster style," said Callum Johnston, storeowner and long-time comic collector.

"Years later, the fellows who took over from him, who emulated his style, set the standard for Tarzan," said Johnston.

In an interview with *The Comics Journal* from September 1985, Foster talks about his youth in Halifax: skipping school to play along the Halifax docks, rafting Tarzan-like on the harbour waters, smelling the different odours of foreign vessels. Interviewed in Florida at age eighty-seven, Foster recalled the original *Bluenose* schooner in his home province. He never forgot us.

He left Nova Scotia

THE HALIFAX ARTIST:
TARZAN WAS HIS FOSTER CHILD.

at age fourteen when his stepfather took the family to Winnipeg in 1906. Always drawing, Foster sketched his own body in the mirror, early training for his near-naked apeman pictures. He quit school to work. First doing clerical duties, later he was a woods guide and even a prize fighter.

But he loved to draw. He rode his bicycle all the way to Chicago to join the Art Institute and later the National Academy of Design at the Chicago Academy of Fine Art.

Beginning as an advertising illustrator, he lived off the Tarzan strip through the years of the Great Depression. According to Foster, he and his young family "ate ape for five or six years."

His unique strip style dropped the cartoon balloon around the text. Foster was illustrating narratives, not drawing cartoons. His long, creative career earned him the coveted cartoonists' prize, the Reuben Award.

In 1937, he left Tarzan and created—ta dah! — Prince Valiant! Remember him?

"They are just great adventure stories, set in the time of King Arthur, and they have dragons and pirates and knights fighting other knights," said Johnston.

"Valiant travelled to the new world and the illustrations are remarkable," he said.

Valiant was hugely popular and Foster drew and wrote the prince's stories for the rest of his life.

"'Prince Valiant' is often referred to as the greatest American comic strip," said Johnston, "because of its quality of illustration and great adventure stories."

Foster's drawing style, and fussy attention to research and detail shaped several graphic greats who followed in his inky footsteps.

"He later influenced Burne Hogarth who went on to form part of the School of Visual Arts in New York."

This Nova Scotian–born artist helped shape the early genre of comic strip realism. "Comic strip artists like Alex Raymond and Milton Caniff and Hal Foster are pretty much the godfathers of the art style of the fine illustration," said Johnston. "Not the cartoon style but more the adventure, somewhat realistic styles," he said.

"Artists like Kurt Swan who defined the look of Superman in the 1960s and 70s and into the 80s, his style I think owes a lot to Hal Foster."

Local comic strip lovers should be proud. "I think it's important for people to know that this fellow was Canadian," said Johnston.

"Certainly for artists and writers working in Nova Scotia, it might be a good little boost to their self-confidence, that this fellow who became world renowned [was from here]."

Students at NSCAD University should take heart.

"He's a little forgotten these days, but during his heyday, he was one of the best-known artists in the world and hailed from Nova Scotia originally," said Johnston.

This is Halifax's illustrious link to illustration greatness! Johnston thinks we should get serious about this master of the funnies. "It would be nice if there might be a little statue of Prince Valiant somewhere just to commemorate that the fellow who created him came from this area," he said.

Brilliant idea! Haligonians should definitely erect a memorial to Foster's noble, courageous prince.

Or at least make a Valiant attempt.

THE WORLD'S SMALLEST NEWSPAPER

Nova Scotia's *Tiny Tattler* was big but little

It was small but mighty. Canada's smallest newspaper sprang from the energies of a fourteen-year-old boy using a hand press in tiny Central Grove on remote Long Island, Digby County. It began in February 1933. Though little and rural, the *Tiny Tattler* gained a readership of five thousand, spread across the world. It boasted national and local advertisers. Old copies are still hoarded by Long and Brier Islanders who still fondly remember the puny publication. In retrospect, its charming motto made a good point: "Who can tell what good may spring from such a tiny little thing?" Much good did follow from this unique periodical.

Originally just ten by fifteen centimetres (four by six inches), the paper grew to a hefty fourteen by twenty centimetres (five and one-half by eight inches) in size. Practically a broadsheet! It lasted only ten years, but it sent Long Island & Brier Island, and Digby Neck news around the world to expatriate Nova Scotians as far as South Africa, Australia, New Zealand, Alaska, and the United States.

The paper's founder, Ivan Shortliffe, grew up on Long Island and became fascinated by rubber stamps and ink as a young boy. The owner and editor of the *Digby Courier*, J. J. Wallis, taught Ivan about the printing process. Then, one year, a special gift from Wallis got young Ivan hooked on the inky-finger business for good.

"At Christmas time, a hand press arrived at his home," said Peggy Shortliffe, Ivan's widow, when I reached her at her home in Truro. "He made a little paper and showed it to his mom and asked if other people would enjoy it," she said.

The *Tiny Tattler* was born. Ivan chose a partner, his best friend, Rupert Cann. Their little paper began to sell. Initial subscriptions were 25¢ for a year; 50¢ in the USA. Locals loved it. Folks living away savoured the news from home.

Despite the *Tattler*'s edgy journalistic slogan—"Without fear or favour!"—harmless neighbourly news filled most of its pages. "Like who was having a birthday party or if there was a dance going on or if someone was visiting relatives," said Mrs. Shortliffe.

Rupert Cann's sister, Winnie Outhouse, still lives on Long Island and remembers how the little *Tiny Tattler* would print all the news that would fit in a newspaper about the size of a person's hand.

"If somebody visited their parents or if someone grew something unusual in the garden or something like that, that would be in it," she said. "If they had a marriage or a death a social occassion."

She's not kidding. Here are some *Tiny Tattler* tidbits. From the June 24, 1937 edition: "Mr. and Mrs. B. Morell enjoyed a motor trip to Yarmouth on Thursday." There's also this: "The first dandelion of the season was found one day last week by Keith Finigan of Freeport."

From the April 8, 1937 edition: "Dr. and Mrs. F. E. Rice of Sandy Cove visited friends in the village on Saturday evening."

Pretty soft stuff. Nevertheless, the two teenage publishers declared this daunting paper policy: "To oppose wrong doing and to uphold with zeal every worthy cause."

Hence, the puny paper had its hard news stories too: Editorials, talk of war preparation, reports on fishermen drowned in storms, how the local fish market was going—those types of things. The young journalistic duo even faced death threats when they ran a story that exposed a rum-running operation.

The printing process was a family affair. "My sister used to set the type," said Winnie Outhouse. The boys had "a little hand press, run by hand, then after a while when the paper became bigger they had a foot press."

Winnie helped with the folding for mailing. The *Tattler* was the smallest newspaper in the world to receive government recognition as second-class mail; it went postage free within a sixty-five kilometre (forty-mile) radius.

Ivan Shortliffe went on to a bigger broadsheet, the *Halifax Herald*. Rupert Cann ran the *Tiny Tattler* until 1943, when he went to war and was forced to stop the presses.

In fact, overseas in a London theatre, some of the Long Island boys in uniform were reminded of their favourite paper back home.

"The newsreel was called 'Did You Know That?'" said Peggy Shortliffe. "The boys were very excited when the *Tiny Tattler* came on the movie screen!"

That newsreel featuring Canada's smallest newspaper was shown around the British Empire with a special screening for the king and queen.

I've seen that old film. It shows the skinny young rural lads entering their little print shop—a wooden shed—and cranking away at the press while also checking copy intently. Cub reporters hard at work.

Ivan Shortliffe stuck with his printing passion his whole life. He worked for bigger newspapers in Halifax, Saint John, Shelburne and Yarmouth. He ended his years writing for the *Halifax Herald* and died in 1978.

The *Tattler* was the smallest paper of his career, but perhaps had the biggest effect on him.

"I think Ivan thought he did it for the people of the islands and surrounding area," said his widow.

"It was a love, something done from his heart; it wasn't a money-making venture," she said.

Today, also from the heart, there is a website run by Ivan Shortliffe's grandchildren. It is their modern-day memorial to his passion for print. At tinytattler.tripod.com, images of his old *Tiny Tattler* newspapers are posted. Thanks to this modern form of publishing technology, people all over the world can now see the tiniest newspaper in the world.

THE FULL-CIRCLE FAMILY

A century later, a Trinidadian Nova Scotian finds his roots

When frozen February sets in and we on this exposed, coastal protuberance jutting into chilled Atlantic waters, muse about sailing south to live, well…who could blame us? It is natural to want to break from our icebound coast to go to where it's hot, hot, hot. That's what a smart, young minister from Scotch Hill, Pictou County did in 1870. But it was no Caribbean vacation. It was a serious life change. He jumped out of the snowbank and into the fire. He was fulfilling a childhood dream by doing mission work abroad; thirty-seven years in the heat of Trinidad and Tobago, off the northern coast of South America.

The West Indies island of Trinidad was awash in desperate East Indian labourers filling the gap left with the abolishment of slavery. However, large, powerful estate owners didn't treat the indentured immigrant labourers much better.

That's why the courageous Presbyterian minister, Rev. Kenneth James Grant, sailed from Nova Scotia, with his brand-new bride, down to the warm climes of Trinidad. He went to set up a mission, to serve the poorest of the poor. But that was his way. His leadership skills shone from a young age while growing up in Scotch Hill.

By fifteen, this bright farm boy had begun teaching school in Pictou County. Educated in Truro and Halifax—and later in the United States—he was a minister first in Merigomish, Pictou County. His southern mission work was in Trinidad's San Fernando area. Rev. Grant rallied the people, built the Susamachar Church, created schools for children and founded a teacher training school called Naparima College—still operating today with a good reputation. That's all very nice. But being nice wasn't what made it happen.

I learned that much from Rev. Grant's great-great-grandson, Ken Taylor, who grew up in Trinidad but, through fluke or fate, came to live in this province. Ken was raised reading the published writings about—and hearing the oral history of—this pious but practical ancestor on his mother's side. He knows the good reverend had no problem taking on the establishment.

"He would certainly have run into a lot of opposition from estate owners," said Ken in his pleasant West Indies accent. "Many did not appreciate his interfering with their workers."

Those workers were essentially slave labour. In the face of that bleak social scene, Rev. Grant was not the stereotypically demure man of the cloth.

"He was stubborn, hard-working, wouldn't take no for an answer," said his great-great-grandson.

"He attended meetings where he would argue with people for better conditions and was not afraid to take on the authorities of the time."

But if you are getting the image of a dour, tight-lipped Victorian-era Presbyterian minister in your mind, forget it. Rev. Grant was also known for his winning smile and a grand sense of humour—a family trait. Photographic portraits of that era are normally stiff, but I'm sure I could see a subtle grin on his face.

Almost four decades of serving the Trinidadians, spiritually and socially, eventually drew to a close. It was time for Rev. Grant to come home. He returned to live in Halifax on Vernon Street and was associated with Fort Massey Church. But, soon he was off again for a while. In his senior years, he served in British Columbia. He helped the East Indian Sikhs emigrating to Canada in the early 1900s before again returning to Halifax. His childhood dream of doing mission work had never faded.

His descendant, Ken Taylor, who grew up in Trinidad, also had childhood visions—dreams about what he imagined to be a magical place: his great-great-grandfather's Nova Scotia. A very old great-aunt, Claudy, had sailed from Nova Scotia down to Trinidad on visits, filling Ken's young head with stories of the family's ancestral homeland.

"She used to tell us about Nova Scotia," said Ken. "To me it was a mysterious place."

He remembers with glee the scramble on the dock as bundles of exotic, green Nova Scotian Christmas trees were off loaded in the warm air for the holiday season.

The Grant family prospered in Trinidad over many years. Yet, for generations, the family's bond with their Nova Scotian homeland was kept alive. One full century after Rev. Grant sailed south in 1870, Ken's family left Trinidad, in the early 1970s. His parents moved with him to Britain. But Ken told me that that didn't feel like home so he left. He travelled. And some sort of personal force pulled him…here, to our shores. It just felt right for him.

"It's my mother's family home so I came here," he said. "I guess I came full circle. I never thought, in my childhood, I'd end up here!"

Once here, he stayed. He made a special trip from Halifax up to Pictou County to see the old family gravestones. He wanted to feel beneath his feet the earth his great-great-grandfather had walked over a century ago, before venturing off to his distant calling in the West Indies. Through some miraculous tug of the heart, some mysterious tightening of the ties that bind, he found himself back in his forefather's homeland. Even after four generations had passed, Ken's family journey had come full circle and he felt welcome. He was home.

HALIFAX'S SECRET TUNNELS: TRUE OR FALSE?

Getting to the bottom of the great tunnel debate, once and for all

Secret military escape tunnels running down from the Citadel Hill fort, under Halifax, and maybe even beneath the harbour floor and out to Georges Island: True? Not true? Wouldn't you love to finally hear the definitive answer?

This rumour/legend/myth/oral tradition has burrowed its way deeply into Halifax's urban imagination. Opinions are equally firm on both sides of this tunnel debate, which resurfaces every so often with no resolution in sight. Speculation—rather than historical proof—has carved out a deep cavity for this tunnel story. It's been around almost a century.

I am told that an elderly woman wrote a letter to the editor of the *Chronicle Herald* some years ago, claiming she had a childhood memory of her father, who worked on Georges Island, taking her down a tunnel that emerged on the city's harbourfront.

In 1976, the *Chronicle Herald* ran a photo of a reporter standing in a dark, arch-roofed, stone walled tunnel that construction workers had unexpectedly discovered beneath Prince Street in downtown Halifax.

According to Dianne Marshall, author of *Georges Island: The Keep of Halifax Harbour*, similar underground tunnels were uncovered in 1973 and 1958, under George Street and beneath Duke Street.

And here's the kicker: Dianne Marshall's book includes an alleged eyewitness account of the underwater tunnel. "He had been contracted by the army to build two tunnels under the streets of Halifax," said Marshall.

His name was John William Cameron, a master mason and contractor from Pictou County who worked in Halifax in the 1860s and 1870s.

"He described those tunnels as having arched ceilings made with slate walls," she said.

Cameron passed this story on to his family. "He told them one tunnel went to the harbour and one tunnel went out to Georges Island," said Marshall, "but he couldn't tell them any more than that because he had been sworn to secrecy."

Do you believe it? Dr. C. Jean Cameron, the mason's great-granddaughter and a Pictou County family physician, certainly believes it. I reached her by phone and by email.

"The family history is just too firm for me to believe otherwise of their existence," she wrote to me.

Speaking as a medical scientist trained to diagnose and make sound judgments based on the facts presented, Dr. Cameron listed a contingent of family members from the last two generations who have all clearly understood this piece of oral tradition to be absolutely true.

Each generation of the Scottish Camerons appointed a keeper of the family history. Dr. Cameron insists this tunnel tale was carefully and truthfully preserved.

"Why would he make it up?" she asked me.

Her ancestor was a no-nonsense Scottish stone mason with the right kind of experience. He worked on stone culvert construction for Canada's new national railway and on Cape Breton's old St. Peter's Canal.

Did John William Cameron help dig a tunnel under Halifax harbour, similar to the famous underwater tunnel beneath the English Channel?

"He had the expertise and competence for the project," said Dr. Cameron. "There is no question that he was in Halifax at the time; he was married there," she said. "He died in 1921."

"He talked about it only as an old man," she said. "He told his grandkids."

NEWSPAPER PHOTO PROVOKED RENEWED TUNNEL TALK.

She ended one email this way: "I will wait for the historians to disprove the hypothesis!"

Well, that's the problem. Historians don't work that way. Usually they assemble what information exists to form a hypothesis rather than wait for one to come along, then work hard to prove or disprove it. That would be backwards research. No, historians usually want a piece of paper or physical proof of some kind. And, in the case of Halifax's mysterious tunnels, there is none. Family hearsay can only go so far.

That's why I took matters into my own hands and set off in search of concrete proof. Or even carved-stone proof. I investigated by getting permission to nose about beneath some old downtown city buildings. I poked about the cellar underneath the Midtown Tavern, next to Prince Street, and in the basement of the Carleton Building block and under the Dennis Building, across from the provincial legislature and next to George Street. I saw old bricked-up entranceways in those stone cellars. Is that proof?

The five historians I consulted in Halifax all say it's wishful thinking. David Flemming, formerly of the Maritime Museum of the Atlantic on Halifax's waterfront, was once in the tunnel in which the *Herald* reporter was photographed. Flemming told me that that tunnel "petered out to a waterpipe."

Dr. Ron McDonald, a Parks Canada historian for Citadel Hill and Georges Island told me those old arched passages are simply old municipal drainage tunnels. Dan Norris, a city official who deals with issues of historic buildings for the Halifax Regional Municipality, agrees with that. He has seen the old underground charts.

Dr. Flemming thinks the blocked-up entranceways I saw in the old cellars were likely just old service entrances that once led up to the sidewalk. Perhaps easy access to unload barrels of supplies from wooden carts, down into cellar storage rooms.

In all his years as a Citadel Hill historian, Dr. McDonald has never seen any Citadel or Georges Island documents about secret escape tunnels. In fact I think he's boggled that the debate refuses to die after all these years. He's puzzled at how hundreds of men digging could have been kept secret from the whole town! And how did they get through all that bedrock? He questions the logic of the tunnel believers.

He acknowledges that there are "countermine" tunnels running part way down Citadel Hill. But they are short and cramped and were intended for placing explosives beneath the grassy slopes to blow up attackers creeping up the hillside on foot. Those passageways didn't even reach the hill's bottom. But visitors to the hilltop fort who saw the entrances to those passageways might have made assumptions that added to the bigger tunnel legend.

Barbara Schmeisser, a highly respected former federal historian for Georges Island, believes an under-the-harbour tunnel would be "unlikely and impractical." She says that somebody's diary or old letter referring to such a tunnel would have surely turned up in the last century. None exists.

My conclusion? In Nova Scotia, old family oral tradition often enlightens the historian's exploration of history's dim corners. And sometimes it leads to a blind end.

HOME-GROWN TURBO POWER!

Our pioneer in turbine technology helped make jet planes possible

Sonic booms from the Concorde airplane once rattled kitchen dishes along the south shore. Seems a Nova Scotian inventor can be blamed for that. He helped develop the turbo-supercharger for aircraft engines, a major engineering breakthrough in flying higher and faster. From Kemptville, Yarmouth County, Waverly A. Reeves was a pioneer of this new, prewar technology.

His 1947 obituary in a Yarmouth newspaper was written from Lynn, Massachusetts, the home of the original General Electric plant where Reeves worked.

He left Nova Scotia at age nineteen with only a grammar-school education, and became a leading engineer at GE, a member of the Jet Pioneers of America, and holder of four patents and two pending in the supercharger field. He also won the Coffin Award, GE's highest honour for employee achievement.

He worked with Dr. Sanford Moss, a leader in perfecting the aircraft engine turbo-supercharger in 1917. In the Turbine Research Department, Reeves designed the apparatus for testing Moss's device that ran at the astonishing 20,000 revolutions per minute. Reeves was nicknamed Pin Wheel and Turbo Bill.

The historian for the General Electric factory in Massachusetts, David Carpenter, author of four books on GE inventions and current president of the Jet Pioneers of America, is impressed with our man Reeves. He told me that, unlike other tests, which were done at sea level, Moss's test happened at a high altitude. That's where this Nova Scotian came in.

"Reeves helped him [Moss] build the test rig and supervised the actual test," said Carpenter.

"So they built this test rig with the Liberty engine and took the turbo-supercharger up to 4,300 metres (14,109 feet), about two-and-a-half miles up," said Carpenter.

In 1918, they were up on Pike's Peak, Colorado, the highest altitude on the continental US. Their engine revved to 356 horsepower, a successful improvement even from ground-level speed. Turbo-chargers compress the thin air of high altitudes to further feed the engine, allowing it to "breathe" better and fly higher.

Waverly Reeves worked forty years at GE, "doing things the practical way," according to his associates. The in-flight test of their design didn't come until July 1937: a test flight of the TWA Gamma, an early over-the-weather aircraft. Waverly Reeves meant to just watch. But the pilot, Tommy Tomlinson, goaded Reeves to come along for the flight.

"Now, Reeves had never flown before," said Carpenter, "but he didn't hesitate, supposedly."

"He hopped in the plane, they showed him how to use the oxygen mask; they were in the baggage compartment." Beside him was a mechanic.

"So, up the plane goes to some 11,278 metres (37,000 feet)," said Carpenter. "They were going to fly from Kansas City to Dayton Ohio." But in mid-flight, something went very wrong.

"About halfway to Dayton, the oxygen mask on the other guy stopped working; he passed out," said Carpenter. "Reeves was trying to get the attention of the pilot but this plane had an open cockpit for the pilot; he couldn't get a hold of him. He tried to get his oxygen mask on the fellow and got some air up the guy's nose and revived him."

"They flew halfway back to Dayton on the buddy system: 'You take a few breaths, I take a few breaths,'" he said.

Our man Reeves saved the mechanic's life and the flight test was a success. Confidence in the supercharger development program got a great boost.

When war struck, Reeves was sent to England in 1941 with the first batch of B-17s to supervise the operation of the turbo-superchargers. From that supercharger technology, jet propulsion evolved. The first jet engine came in time for war.

GE was secretly working on Frank Whittle's jet engine design from England. Reeves, as a member of the Jet Pioneers, would have been part of that historic military, scientific project.

"He was in on that secret engine project before it flew in 1942," said Carpenter. "The secret was that we had a jet engine and it was the same secrecy as the Manhattan Project, the atom bomb."

But Reeves and Moss themselves were actually first with a jet engine design years previously— they just didn't know it!

They pretty much had the design on paper, but calculations told them it would fail if built. So it remained on the drawing board.

"They had two-thirds of a jet engine," said Carpenter, excitedly. "They had the compressor, they had the turbine, all you need is hot air but they just didn't do it! And after the war, everybody and his brother was making jet engines out of turbo-superchargers. It [the Reeves and Moss design] was almost there!"

Waverly Reeves was a pioneer in turbo technology from our own backyard. By the 1930s, as his career in airplane engine design was soaring to great heights, Reeves revisited his childhood stomping grounds of Yarmouth County. He didn't forget where he was from. But in the fascinating new field of turbo-powered engines, he sure was going places.

THE TWISTED MYSTERIES
OF A WAR ARTIST

Uncovering odd links to the life of a great Canadian painter

Gyrth Russell was a young, gifted artist from Nova Scotia who painted lovely, soft landscapes and marinescapes all his life, but early in his career he helped the world to see and to feel the devastation of World War One. As a kid in his twenties, selected by Lord Beaverbrook, he was, briefly, a Canadian war artist in 1917. He captured on canvas the muddied wasteland left by Canada's horrific but triumphant battle for Vimy Ridge in France.

Born in 1892, he was the youngest child of a justice of the Nova Scotian Supreme Court, Benjamin Russell, and Louise Coleman Russell. The family lived in Dartmouth but moved to Morris Street in Halifax. Russell grew up sketching the Halifax waterfront. He was part of the Canadian revival of the art of etching at the turn of the last century. By age twenty, he was gone from Nova Scotia and from Canada more or less for good. He chose to settle in England and Wales after the war. His work is in esteemed collections in Britain and elsewhere.

One Canadian art expert called him "mysterious" in a 1997 article in *Artsatlantic* magazine.

Dr. Allan Quigley, a great-nephew of this artist, stumbled across the puzzling article the day he arrived in Nova Scotia from Western

Canada. It was an odd twist in fate. While he was being interviewed for his job at St. Francis Xavier University, in Antigonish, his wife, an artist, happened to spy that very magazine at the campus gallery.

"The name Gyrth caught her eye," said Quigley. "Here's this article: 'The Mysterious Mr. Russell.' What are the odds that we would be in Antigonish, that she'd be in the art gallery, that she'd pick up this very issue and that we'd know who this guy was?"

It seemed a prophetic twist in family fate.

"He was my great-uncle, so it all came together."

But why the label "mysterious"?

Quigley certainly knew about the artist's life. It seems the Ottawa art expert who penned the piece found Russell's available bio information a bit thin. Although Russell's art showed in Canada and some of his paintings are carefully kept here, he remained distant from his home and homeland.

However, Russell's biography is being prepared by Susan Flint, in England. Her letter to me explains that the painter for many years had entries in *Who's Who* and in several dictionaries of artists. She contends there is no mystery about the man. He did not return to Canada after 1923, she says, simply because of "the lack of soft colouring which he loved so much in Britain."

**A BRUSH WITH FAME:
NOVA SCOTIA'S GYRTH RUSSELL**

Quigley and his artistic wife, Linda, did briefly meet this Canadian war artist once, just before he died, in 1970. As travelling students, they visited Russell's home in Wales.

"He was a charming, diminutive little man," said Quigley.

Despite his short time capturing on canvas the worst the world had to offer, Russell was a happy little man in old age.

"Maybe five feet tall, flowing white hair, wonderful sense of humour, a good sense of the absurd," said Quigley. "He lived in the apartment with his wife, retired and surrounded by poodles."

When a younger Russell had left Nova Scotia, already married to the first of three wives, he studied art in Boston and later in Paris. Russell's works were shown in the Canadian War Memorials exhibit in London in 1919 and later in Ottawa, Toronto, and widely shown across America and Britain. His original war drawings are now in the Imperial War Museum in London.

The older, retired Russell gave the young Quigley a couple of paintings in 1970, but that magazine article nearly thirty years later spawned a yearning in him to see more of his great-uncle's art. In Ottawa, Quigley went to Canada's war museum and talked his way into their art vault. He stood, surrounded by eighteen of his great-uncle's grand paintings.

"They're quite large and in the impressionist mode," he said. "They're quite lovely."

For more reasons than one, the experience was "quite stunning."

"Here's a man we met but didn't really know and here's a link through art—my wife's an artist," said Quigley.

He was impressed by "how really wonderful the paintings are. If you want to get the feel of Vimy Ridge or some place in France during the war, I've never seen anything better," he said. "I was awestruck." For Quigley, the paintings have a "forlorn, melancholy sort of feeling, not a harsh feeling; not something that is terrifying."

"It is a sad statement that you see," he said. "He was a total master of the feel of it."

Our own Art Gallery of Nova Scotia has a number of this artist's works in its vault. And here's a neat discovery: the new wing of the AGNS backs on to Bedford Row, where an old Halifax city directory for the time lists an address for this artist, separate from his Morris Street home address. It seems this Nova Scotian gallery that preserves the paintings of this Nova Scotian artist sits on the site of his early Halifax art studio! Another mysterious twist in the story of the painter, Gyrth Russell.

PORTIA WHITE
AND THE TAIL GUNNER

A war vet and a famous contralto musically reunite after fifty years

---

You went away, I had to stay,
Nothing to do but to wait and to pray,
That there will be a meeting,
An old-time rendezvous,
When everything is over,
I'm waiting for you.

I t's odd to think that such lovely lyrics could result from a deadly
wartime plane crash and also lead to a musical meeting between a
young airman and a famous concert singer, but that is exactly what
happened. It's quite a story.

Clifton Outhouse of Tiverton, Long Island, off the tip of Digby Neck,
Nova Scotia, was a twenty-two-year-old tail gunner during the war. He
was flying in a Lancaster Bomber over Germany in 1943. Badly shot up,
the plane sputtered back to England but crash-landed in a farm.

"It killed four up front and threw me out and busted me up quite a
bit," said the eighty-year-old veteran when we spoke at his home.

Broken and bruised, Clifton spent six months in a British hospital,
then more months in an RCAF convalescent home near Toronto. That's

PORTIA WHITE: GAVE AN INJURED AIRMAN'S SONG NEW LIFE.

where the injured airman met another injured flyer, Lew Watt, a gifted piano player from western Canada. The two young men became hospital buddies. Intrigued by Watt's facility with made-up melodies, Clifton joined in the music making. "We sat down and we wrote the words to this song," he said.

His friend Lew couldn't read or write music. "But as fate would have it," said Clifton, "one of the nurses had a degree in music and he played it and she wrote the notes."

They called it "Waiting for You." The whole hospital loved it, especially the commanding officer. He took the injured, uniformed airmen, hobbling with their canes, down to Maple Leaf Gardens in Toronto. The two amateur songwriters were escorted backstage, holding their handwritten musical score.

"We walked into the dressing room and here's this beautiful, very dignified lady sitting there in an evening gown," said Clifton.

The two young men were introduced to Portia White, the internationally famous concert singer.

"I guess she mentioned or I mentioned that we each came from Nova Scotia, but that was it," he said.

Portia White, the highly accomplished contralto singer from Truro, Nova Scotia, studied and sang in Halifax before performing live across Canada and in New York, South America and Europe. She was a big star.

She took the airmen's songsheet and hummed a few bars. That night, the world-renowned performer sang their song in front of six thousand people at Maple Leaf Gardens with the wounded airmen sitting on stage beside her, amazed. The CBC's Lorne Greene was the big-voiced master of ceremonies.

"We were introduced to the audience," said Clifton, "and Portia White got up and sang. Now that was the high point of my memory right there. She sang so beautifully, it was something I know I will never forget."

This mild-mannered gent with the calm, welcoming demeanour has kept that original score all these years. He agreed to mail it to me as I researched this story, and I secretly set about giving his song new life.

Through the assistance of music producer Glenn Meisner at CBC Radio, I arranged to have the wartime love song recorded for the first time. The singer? The late Portia White's younger sister, Yvonne White, a local singer who still performs for veterans in a Halifax hospital. She loved the melody and gave the pretty ballad new wings with her rich, formal, operatic voice, hitting the high notes with a spirit-stirring clarity reminiscent of her famous sister. Nostalgic, romantic, and wonderful, the wartime love song was reborn in a voice eerily similar to the late Portia White's pure sound.

In Clifton Outhouse's living room in Tiverton, I surprised the veteran with a CD recording of Yvonne's performance. He put it in his stereo and pushed the play button. His song, written over half a century before, flowed through the modern stereo speakers.

Standing there speechless, Clifton was hearing his old wartime love song sung in that graceful classical style again, for the first time in fifty-seven years. What a moment. He listened intently and smiled as he recognized his old lyrics:

If it be for ever,
My heart knows what to do,
Keep your memory ever,
I'm waiting for you...

As the last note of his beautiful ballad trailed off, the veteran's eyes watered slightly. For a brief instant, it was 1944 again.

But each long night I pray dear,
That soon the news will come,
The news that we're all hoping for,
That heartaches and sorrows are over and done.
So 'til you're back again dear,
When dreams will all come true,
You will find me waiting,
Forever, for you.

The gentle veteran's first reaction was a soft "Thank you, that was lovely." He was touched. Then his response flowed gleefully:

"My, she has a beautiful voice. You know, when Portia White sang it she had a rich voice like her, almost the same. Isn't that wonderful? Fifty-seven years ago. I can almost see Lew sitting at the piano playing that. He had the talent, he had that beautiful music in his head and he just played it. It certainly turned out well. I…I didn't realize until now that since Lew is gone it really is my song isn't it? Well, I'm going to keep that real close. It brought me back while it was playing. I could almost see him sitting there. It was in the spring because I had my summer uniform on. That's a long while ago. That's the hard part of it; it only seems like yesterday that happened. Well, that's great."

It was truly a magical musical moment for the veteran, standing there lost in memories stirred by song. I could see it in his eyes. He had saved those sweet lyrics all those years. Hearing them again, sung in that eloquent voice, gave him pause. For a minute, he was back in another time, six decades ago.

[...A BONUS!]

THE WATERFALL HUNTER

The passion and power of our remote cascades
and the men who love them

Deep in our forest primeval, crashing cascades of cold river water spill and splash in a roar of white noise. The loudly soothing sound and the glittering spectacle of a waterfall is an unending drama staged at many remote points along numerous Nova Scotian rivers. But how many are out there? Robert Saulnier, a thirty-something industrial scale salesman, is determined to somehow track down and photograph every one. He's already hiked and climbed through wet and wild woods to reach forty-nine falls. They are not all documented on provincial maps but research tells him there are more than a hundred. And he's still looking.

We met at his Halifax apartment where his framed waterfall photos were all over the walls: stunning shots of peace and grandeur. Rushing cascades, caught in mid motion. High gorge walls, lined with overhanging spruce and colourful fall leaves.

He's not a big fitness buff, but some years ago Robert just grew intrigued and began searching for waterfalls by book, map, and word of mouth. His goal was to hike to each one of them.

Some falls are well-known, some rarely seen. For example, a Nova Scotia atlas lists a waterfall in Colchester County by Otter Brook, below

Bentley Lake. When Saulnier asked around, local residents had never heard of it. So he went waterfall hunting.

"After three and a half hours trudging through the woods in hip waders, snow up to my hips, I found them," he said as we talked at his place. "There are seven waterfalls on this brook, all within 400 metres (1,300 feet) of each other in a series of cascades!"

Imagine coming across that wild watery site of raw nature.

"It must be about eighty feet down in this gorge," he said, "they range in height from about thirty feet down to fifteen."

It sounds well worth the walk, especially for a committed waterfall lover.

Some of our falls are small and charming—Burnside Falls between Truro and New Glasgow is just one and one-third metres (four and one-half feet) high—but some are towering and deadly. Our highest waterfall, at thirty-one metres (103 feet), is on North River, behind Baddeck, Cape Breton. Drysdale Falls near Tatamagouche, at twenty metres (sixty-five feet) high, roars down a 350 million-year-old fault line. It is unsafe and off limits. People have been badly hurt there.

The precarious and dangerous Annandale Falls is in Cumberland County, east of the Wentworth valley. Saulnier decided to photograph it so he hiked there with an eighteen-metre (sixty-foot) rope and began descending along the gorge wall.

"As it turned out I was about twenty feet short of rope climbing down into it," said Saulnier.

"I realized that when I got to the end of the rope," he said, "and I'm hanging by one arm, going, 'Yikes!'"

He managed to slip his camera bag off his shoulder and then slide down to the ground along the steep bank. He jumped down, took out his camera and snapped some dramatic shots of the falls.

"Then I pondered my dilemma after I took the pictures." He hadn't planned on how to get back up! Now, there's a passionate hobbyist! A dead tree leaning against the gorge wall did the trick. He climbed it to reach his dangling rope again.

Why risk life and limb to capture these roaring rivers on film? Well, you'd have to be there.

"I think it is a combination of the beauty of the water cascading over the rocks, and the white noise," he said, thoughtfully.

"It's very soothing and relaxing. I could be hiking in the woods for hours trying to find one of these and once I get to it, I am in awe of the beauty."

Or maybe there's something about these moving waters that attracts us physiologically. I asked another published waterfall researcher about that theory.

"There are scientific minds that say there are negative ions that are released from moving water," said Billard, author of Waterfalls of Nova Scotia.

He's right. Microscopic negative ions of oxygen are said to help you breathe easier and so feel refreshed and energized.

"The splashing and high activity generated create negative ions in the air that affect your state of mind," said Billard.

They are like tiny vitamins in the air, you might say.

The power of waterfalls is also financial. Billard writes about the waterfall on the Mersey River, now a power dam where early electrification in Queen's County began. Some people tried to dam White Rock Falls on the Avon River, near Windsor. It was Nova Scotian entrepreneur Roy Jodrey who finally harnessed its power in order to sell kitchen appliances.

"He ended up with all kinds of power, more than needed for his little refrigerator-sales business," said Billard.

Instead, Jodrey built and ran pulp mills. Then he accumulated lots of land, "Because he needed land for the reservoirs behind these dams for the power generation," said Billard.

"He became a real industrial baron in Nova Scotia, all based on that one success in a waterfall."

There you have it. Nova Scotia's wonderful waterfalls: a story of powerful passion and a passion for power.

PHOTO CREDITS

p.8: Cumberland County Museum and Archives

p.12: Archival and Special Collections, McLaughlin Library, University of
Guelph, L. M. Montgomery Collection

p.20: John Simpkin Collection

p.27: Loré Family Collection

p.29: Shelburne County Museum

p.32: Mayme Morrison Brown

p.48: Ed Jacobs Collection

p.54: Lee Family Collection

p.68: Bob McNeil Collection

p.83: John Soosaar Collection

p.97: L. B. Jenson

pp.100, 103, 105: Bruce Nunn Collection

p.106: Copyright 2003 Julianne MacLean. All rights reserved.
Reproduction with the permission of the publisher, Harlequin Books S.A.

p.108: Charles E. Doucet

p.114: Icelandic Society of Nova Scotia

p.117: Vivian Thomas Collection

p.123: University College of Cape Breton

p.127: Halifax Herald Ltd.

p.130: Dalhousie University Archives, Dalhousie University Photograph
collection, PC1, Box 6, Folder 32

p.133: Dalhousie University Archives, Archibald MacMechan collection,
MS-2-82, C549

p.134: Rockwell Kent

p.146: Oakville Museum

p.147: Nancy Hart Collection

p.151: Vesta Mosher Collection

p.154: Chuck Lapp Collection

p.165: Dartmouth Heritage Museum

p.189: Halifax Herald Ltd.

p.195: Allan and Linda Quigley Collection